The Platinum Rule®
FOR
SALES MASTERY

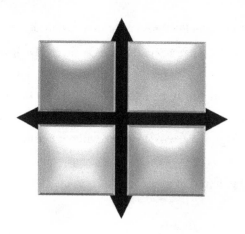

DR. TONY ALESSANDRA
SCOTT MICHAEL ZIMMERMAN
and DR. JOSEPH LA LOPA

◼ PLATINUM RULE PRESS
PLATINUM RULE GROUP, LLC.

The Platinum Rule®

FOR SALES MASTERY

ISBN: 978-0-9832989-4-6 (Hardcover)
ISBN: 978-0-9819371-2-0 (Paperback)
ISBN: 0-000000-00-0 (Audio)
ISBN: 978-0-9819371-5-1 (eBook)

Published by:

 **PLATINUM RULE PRESS**

Platinum Rule Group, LLC.
600 31st Street SW
Barberton, Ohio 44203
1-330-848-0444
www.PlatinumRule.com

Cover & Interior Design by:
Glenn Griffiths
www.TheCyranoGroup.com

ACKNOWLEDGEMENTS

WE ARE GRATEFUL TO ALL OF THE PSYCHOLOGISTS, sociologists, visionaries, philosophers, coaches, consultants, trainers, speakers and authors who directly and indirectly influenced our work, documented their findings and who built foundations of evidence upon which we could build. Just a sampling of these include: Michael J. O'Connor, Katherine Briggs, Jim Cathcart, Roger Dawson, John Geier, Paul Green, Phil Hunsaker, Carl Jung, Florence Littauer, Russ Watson, William Moulton Marston, David McClelland, David Merrill, Roger Reid, Larry Wilson, Bill Schwarz, Isabel Briggs Myers, Don Lowry, Janice Van Dyke and Don Hutson.

We wish to thank our clients for providing us with encouragement, financial support, opportunities to fail forward (and grow in the process) and for challenging our thinking.

We want to say a special thanks to Glenn Griffiths for the wonderful graphic design he provided for this book and for his continuing contributions to The Platinum projects.

A big tip of the hat to Dan Alsip and Alan Brunton for reading the manuscript with critical eyes and open minds, and for asking us all the right questions.

Our deepest gratitude goes to our colleague and friend, Rick Barrera. Many of the sales concepts in the Section IV chapters of this book were developed since 1986 in conjunction with Rick Barrera, the co-author, with Tony Alessandra, of *Non-Manipulative Selling* and *Collaborative Selling* and the author of the best-selling book, *Overpromise and Overdeliver*.

what others have said about
THE PLATINUM RULE

"The ability to communicate effectively with others is the key to success and happiness. Tony Alessandra has [created] the most important, practical, and effective [concept] ever imagined."
– **Brian Tracy**, Author, *Maximum Achievement*

"The Platinum Rule is a must for all of us who want to be better in our interactions with others." – **Ken Blanchard**, Co-author,
The One-Minute Manager and *Raving Fans*

"Apply [these ideas] to your own activities, each day, and watch your career and your life change for the better" – **Og Mandino**,
Author/ Speaker

"The Platinum Rule breaks all the old rules of communications ... cuts like a laser to the heart of the human personality ... yours and your customer's ... it's a learning and earning tool for the times."
– **Harvey Mackay**, Author,
Swim with the Sharks Without Being Eaten Alive

"Dr. Tony Alessandra's work brilliantly provides effective insights for improving communication in any and all situations."
– **John Gray**, Ph.D., Author,
Men Are From Mars, Women Are From Venus

DEDICATIONS

I dedicate this book to my late father, Victor Alessandra, who taught me the "street smarts" that helped me become successful in selling, in business and in life. **— TONY ALESSANDRA**

Sweet P, my one and only: thank you for sharing your life with me. Mom, thanks for always giving me just enough and making me work for the rest. Big Jim, bless you for walking the righteous walk (I miss you every day). Father Norm Douglas and Larry Vuillemin: thanks for spending the time teaching me MBTI, the Enneagram and for jump-starting my inner journey. To Bosko, thank you for breathing life into Cyrano; you are a true genius. Mick, thanks for sharing your ideas, experiences and energy with me. Tony, thank you for letting me share in your greatest discovery: The Platinum Rule, and for providing me with guidance, confidence and opportunities. **— SCOTT ZIMMERMAN**

This book is dedicated to my father and mother for their unconditional love and support, which has helped me cope with the high and low points of my life, and to my wife and children, who inspire me every day to be a better person, father, husband, and teacher. I also want to thank Tony Alessandra and Scott Zimmerman for making my dream of writing a book like this one come true. **— MICK LA LOPA**

TABLE OF CONTENTS

INTRODUCTION

THELMA, DEREK AND ROGER HAD BEEN SEATED FOR fifteen minutes when Suzie burst into the restaurant.

While chatting into her cell phone, Suzie looked around, spotted her associates, smiled and waved as she bounced over to the table.

Even though she was late, the other three silently forgave her the moment she sat down. It was nearly impossible to stay mad at Suzie; she was truly likeable and oozed charm.

Suzie snapped her cell phone shut and offered a half-hearted apology. "I'm so sorry about the time, but I just left the most exciting brainstorming session... *ever!*" she gushed. Suddenly, she noticed a server silently waiting for her to pick up the menu; the rest of the group had long since placed their order. After some friendly banter with the waitress, she ordered. Then, she turned back and asked, "What was I just talking about?"

Roger helped her out by saying, "You were talking about the great meeting you just left."

Derek quickly interjected, "Suzie, I know you're about to regale us with another epic tale, but we really need to get down to business. I need to make my final decision about which marketing firm we are going to hire. I have a two-fifteen appointment, and because of Suzie's tardiness, we're already twenty minutes late. You have all interviewed the representatives from four competing marketing firms; give me your recommendations and reasoning for the firm you each think I should hire.'"

Roger offered Suzie a sympathetic glance as if to apologize for Derek's remark. Suzie smiled as if to say, "No sweat, I'm over it already."

"I saved the original requirements we agreed upon before we began

I

the interviewing process, and I made a point to bring a copy for everyone," Thelma added.

After Derek quickly glanced over Thelma's spreadsheet, he commented, "I'll start. From my brief interviews with the candidates, Michael seemed to grasp the big picture the quickest. He shared with me specific results he expects to get, and I liked his confidence in his ability to help us grow sales and increase client retention. The other candidates lacked focus, seemed indecisive or flat-out wasted my time with details that aren't relevant to my goals. Plus, I think it would take them too long to get up to speed about how I like things done around here. So, unless there are any reasons not to hire Michael, I'm ready to make a decision and move forward. Anyone disagree?"

Suzie jumped in on the conversation, "I'm glad you think that Michael is our guy, Derek. I found him to be very quick on his feet; he and I hit it off right away. I shared with him a couple of my ideas for growing sales and he gave examples about how some of them worked with his other clients. He also added some of his own visions that were in alignment with my ideas. He said he would help me list and prioritize my ideas, so we could initially concentrate on the top one or two that would make the greatest impact. Besides, have you seen the companies Michael is working with? Talk about heavy hitters! I have some friends at some of those firms and called them to find if they liked working with Michael's team. They all praised him and highly recommended his company. I'm sold."

During the brief moment of silence, Roger collected his thoughts and then quietly added, "I'm so glad that he suggested that we prioritize your ideas before blindly plunging forward. Our staff is still adjusting to the changes our last consultant recommended. In fact, I'm still not sure if some of those changes were even necessary. From all the candidates I met, Michael seemed the most sincere about helping me support the team and putting together a win-win agreement. I can tell that he truly wants to help us achieve our goals."

Roger continued, "I drove over to their offices, and I was able to meet his team. Michael recommended that I talk to his staff members individually; I wanted to obtain a better impression of how we might work together, how each supports their team, and how their team helps companies like ours. His staff seemed very dedicated and they obviously respected and trusted Michael. Oh, and another thing that really impressed me about Michael was his listening skills. He continually reassured me that any changes we would make would be well thought through and that he would help me justify all the reasons to our team, just so that everyone will feel comfortable with them. So, I guess what I'm trying to say is that my gut feeling tells me that Michael is the best candidate. Although a couple of the other candidates did have some great qualities, I felt Michael was the best. Before I make my final recommendation though, I'm curious about Thelma's thoughts."

Roger shifted his gaze from Derek to Thelma. "What do you think about Michael? Didn't you mention he had some technology that could help us follow-up new leads as well as improve customer communications? What did you think about that?"

Derek quickly looked at his watch and interrupted, "Thelma, make it quick. I have that appointment with a new prospect, and I can't be late. This could be another big project for us. First, just answer 'yes' or 'no'… do we hire Michael?"

Thelma began to respond, "Well, I took it upon myself to do an analysis of all the candidates and their strengths and weaknesses…" Thelma peeked up from her spreadsheet at Derek, noticed his impatience and caught herself, "and uh, I guess to answer your question, Derek, yes, I think that Michael's firm is our best option. I discovered from my research that Michael has a system; a proven process and timesaving technology that facilitate predictable sales growth. He never once mentioned any creative concepts like the prototypical 'ad man.' Michael was very logical and clearly explained each component of his process. He began our second meeting by showing me how traditional marketing and lead acquisition strategies were losing effectiveness in today's information age. He then demonstrated how target marketing, behavior adaptability training and delivering need-specific, timely and customized marketing messages would be more effective than 'shotgun' advertising strategies."

Thelma noticed Derek squirming in his seat and sped up. "Michael stayed focused on what we wanted to accomplish; the others either spun stories or tried to 'hard sell' me. He explained in detail how his methods would lead us, step-by-step, to our goals…"

Derek interrupted once again, "Well it looks like everyone is in agreement. Michael is our man. Time is money; I've gotta run. You all can stay if you like and discuss it further. But for me, I heard all I need to hear."

Roger, wanting to reduce the tension from Derek's interruption, said, "Derek, I can understand that you are in a hurry… it sounds like you have an important meeting. Do you think it might be wise to postpone this decision until Thelma can tell you about the new technology Michael showed her?"

Derek replied, "No, that's not that important to me. If the cost of the technology is too much, I'm sure I can get him to come down in price to fit our budget, or we'll shelve that part until next year. If this next meeting goes the way I expect, the money won't be an issue, anyways. You can stay here if you want to keep hashing this out, but I have to go. Suzie, give Michael a call today and let him know that he is hired. Oh, and have him call Thelma to work through the details of his proposal. Roger, once the details are handled, you can introduce him around to the rest of our staff and make him feel at home… you're good at that 'warm and fuzzy' stuff. I'm going to be out of town for a couple of days, so tell Michael I want to meet when I get back. Lunch is on me; enjoy!"

With that, Derek, plopped down the company credit card and told Thelma to handle the check, add a tip and put the receipt in his in-box. With that, Derek was gone.

Roger asked, "Am I the only one to notice something?"

"What's that?" Thelma asked.

"We've all worked for Derek for at least five years, and this is the first time that we've all been in complete agreement about the same decision."

"Not only did I notice," Suzie said, "but, I can't wait to learn to sell like Michael does. I wanted to hire him within the first five minutes of our first meeting. I don't know what he did, but it sure worked."

"Nothing gets past me," said Thelma. "Just from our lunch conversation, I gleaned several new pieces of information. Michael sold Derek on getting results and gaining an edge over our competitors. Suzie sold herself on the fact that he would help turn her ideas into reality. Michael sensed that Roger needed a feeling of security in the relationship, so he introduced him to his whole team. Finally, he showed me logical thinking and a turnkey process, including technology and training. He never tried to push me into any decision; he gave me information and allowed me to arrive at my own conclusions. I find it amazing that he could determine our 'hot buttons' and match benefits of his services to our specific interests. In essence, he figured out how each of us was going to buy and presented his solutions to each of us in a different manner."

"From my point of view," Thelma continued, "Michael lead each of us down a different path and pointed out different sights along the way, and yet each one of us arrived at the same destination… a decision to do business with his company. However, I know that I made the right decision to hire him, and I never once felt like I was 'being sold.'"

"I totally agree, Thelma." Roger nodded earnestly as he spoke, "You know how I cannot stand high-pressure salespeople. Michael never once asked me about awarding the contract to his firm; I felt like I was buying; not being asked to buy. It may not sound like much, but it is a huge difference from my perspective. He was completely focused on our needs and goals, not what he wanted. I *wanted* to give him our business, and I was relieved when Derek had arrived at the same conclusion that I had."

Suzie looked up sheepishly and said, "Don't ever tell Derek this, but if we had gone with another firm, I was going to enroll in Michael's sales training classes on my own. I've dealt with dozens of salespeople in my day, but this guy had charisma in spades. I would love to learn more about how he 'connected' with each one of us to make this sale!"

"Beats me," Roger mused. "If you stop and think about it, the four of us couldn't be more different from one another. What I mean to say is that we make a great team, but we really are diverse in our opinions and our approaches to ideas and changes. How in the world did Michael get all four of us to agree on something this important?"

The answer is that Michael identified the behavioral style of each decision maker. He then shifted the speed of his selling process and the focus of the conversation to match the different buying styles of Derek, Suzie, Roger and Thelma.

This book will give you a clear indication of your natural selling style, as well as how you naturally connect with *one* of the four buying styles. More importantly, you will learn how to adapt your selling style to connect with the other three styles (the ones that you may have been losing as customers).

When you learn to adapt your selling style to each prospect's buying style, people will like you, buy from you and refer others to you.

While this example may seem a little farfetched, it actually isn't. In fact, as you delve deeper into this book, you will read about a situation where one of the authors landed an account in a very similar manner. You see, Platinum Rule Selling is a matching process: matching the right product or service to the corresponding set of customer needs, matching the sales pace to the customer's buying pace, and matching your selling style to the buying style of every customer. The ability to adapt your style to your customers' styles helps you build rapport and develop strong relationships.

Your internal voice may be whispering to you, "Isn't it being manipulative when a sales professional adjusts his or her style to match a prospect's?"

Our answer is an emphatic, "No!" To understand why this isn't manipulation, let's stop and consider a wise piece of advice that has been passed along many generations:

"Do unto others as you would have them do unto you."

You may remember this as "The Golden Rule," and it is a great rule to live by. We believe in it 110%, especially when it comes to honesty, values, ethics and having consideration for the needs of others.

However, when it comes to interpersonal communication, it can backfire because others may not wish to be treated the same way you like to being treated.

When Tony Alessandra was a young man, he learned this lesson first-hand when he moved from New York to San Diego. He practiced The Golden Rule verbatim by treating the people in San Diego the way he liked to be treated… as a New Yorker. He came on too strong; he was too assertive and just "too fast" for most of the laid-back people on the West Coast. He rubbed many people the wrong way, which prompted them to "dig in their heels" and few responded positively to his requests.

Fortunately, he soon realized that people are diverse and each need to be treated differently. As he became more self-aware, he coined the phrase, "The Platinum Rule," which states:

*"Do unto others as **they** would have **you** do unto **them**."*

The Platinum Rule is a more sensitive version of the ancient axiom. That is, learn to understand the behaviors of others and interact with them in a style that is best for them, not just for you.

You need to adapt so that, while retaining your own identity, you can lead others in the way they like to follow, speak to them the way they are comfortable listening and sell to them the way they prefer to buy.

When you understand your own style and how it differs from the styles of others, you can adapt your approach to stay "on the same wavelength" with them. Your ideas do not have to change, but you can change the way you present your ideas. We call this adaptability.

Adaptable people realize there is a difference between their inner self (who they are) and their external behavior (how they choose to act). Adaptability is simply changing your behavior, not your personality, values or beliefs. Adaptable people consciously decide to modify their behaviors to a particular person, a situation, or an event. Less adaptable people, on the other hand, respond in a more habitual manner, regardless of whether the response is likely to be appropriate or effective.

When you treat people the way they want to be treated, you are paying attention to their needs, wants and expectations. You are trying to walk in their shoes, to understand their feelings, see their point of view and identify their purchasing requirements. That builds trust, friendship and respect ... three requirements for any strong relationship.

Getting along with others is the universal key to success. In fact, studies have shown that the ability to build rapport with others was the one thing all highly successful people have in common. Mastery of The Platinum Rule is the key to opening the door to successful relationships in all areas of your life... beyond a successful career in sales.

To apply The Platinum Rule, you need to understand how people want to be treated; this requires a basic understanding of personal style and behavior. Throughout the ages, philosophers and psychologists have developed various models to explain these key differences. The guide presented here will give you a powerful tool to help you build rapport with your prospects, customers, colleagues and referral partners. We have based our model on years of research and validation; yet it is simple, practical, and easy to use and remember. We make it easy to identify the preferred style of your customers, associates, friends and family members.

Note: One of the strengths of The Platinum Rule is that we have taken a very complex behavioral and psychological concept and made it relatively easy to understand. However, we also know that "understanding" and "application" are two different outcomes. Therefore, we have purposely mixed spaced repetition with a variety of stories, examples and exercises to reinforce critical points throughout this book. You may experience occasional thoughts of, "Didn't they already tell me that?" as you read, but we encourage you to stop reading during those moments and really give meaningful thought to each concept we want you to "own and apply."

Section I describes the four general behavioral styles of your customers, and it helps you understand your own behavior style and know what type of sales position best matches your natural behaviors. We also identify specific customer buying patterns and the preferences for each style.

If you have never taken an accurate test to help you understand your behavioral style, you should visit www.PlatinumRule.com/assessment to help you identify and understand your own behavioral style. Understanding your own strengths and weaknesses is the first step toward increased self-awareness. Heightened self-awareness of your behaviors, and how they relate to others, will forever change your approach to selling.

Section II describes the two basic behavioral dimensions and gives you a simple process of elimination to help you identify the behavioral style of yourself and your customers. It will also show you how to observe your customer's environment and behaviors to locate other clues that help you determine their behavioral style.

Section III describes how to reduce "relationship tension" to help you establish and maintain rapport with customers. This requires behavioral adaptability on your part, so you can easily connect with those who have styles that are different from your own. You will not learn ways to manipulate others; you will learn skills that anyone working in sales should possess in order to identify and satisfy other's needs to help them grow their business… and yours.

Section IV teaches you about the basic selling steps; how to build on each step to help each buyer reach a successful conclusion. The five steps to sales success are:

1. CONNECTING: This is the critical first step that begins the process of building a customer relationship. When the prospect learns that the salesperson sincerely has his interests at heart, the rest of the sales process continues without obstacles. Once prospects begin to trust you, they will feel more comfortable about sharing their business goals, challenges and shortcomings. When rapport (based on trust and respect) is established, you can begin a process of exploring ways to help them grow and prosper.

2. EXPLORING: For a salesperson well on their way to mastery of **The Platinum Rule**, discovering the needs and wants of the prospect is a top priority. They explore the prospect's situation for needs, opportunities and ideas about how to help move them toward achieving goals or solving problems.

3. COLLABORATING: The Platinum Rule salesperson gets their customers involved in the process of determining the best product or service solution. They collaborate to find a custom-tailored solution to the meet prospect's needs.

4. CONFIRMING: For the most effective salespeople, gaining a firm commitment from a customer or prospect is often just a formality. When the process of exploring for the right solution has been a joint effort, gaining a commitment is a natural outcome. Still, this stage is a critical part of cementing the customer-salesperson partnership; *both* parties need to *confirm* specific commitments each are making to the sale and the delivery of the products and/or services.

5. ASSURING: Assuring customer satisfaction is the last phase of the sales process, and it is the secret to long-term, extraordinary success in selling. Although many salespeople stop after getting the sales commitment, **Platinum Practitioners** ensure each customer receives service, training, installation and maintenance that exceed their expectations.

Section IV will also help you understand how to use each step to build your customer relationship. By thoroughly understanding your customer's style and the five basic selling steps, you will build stronger relationships and turn the sales process into a natural flow... culminating in a "win-win" solution.

The Platinum Rule for Sales Mastery is different from any other methodology used by salespeople today. The Platinum Rule for Sales Mastery is not relationship or personal selling, where the goal is to personalize the relationship between seller and buyer in order for the salesperson to uncover the needs of the customer then offer products and services to satisfy those needs. We are challenging you to master one of the most reliable methods for identifying the Behavioral Style of your customers, and how to sell to them the way they would like to be sold... **not** the way you want to sell them (which is based on your own natural style).

Consider this: there are four behavioral styles and you have *one* of them. If you sell to all your customers based on the way you like to buy then you are only connecting with those who share your style. What this suggests is that you are not connecting with the three other styles; greatly limiting your sales potential. We believe that if you read this book, do the activities, and learn to adapt the way you sell to the way each customer buys, you will become more successful. Additionally, if you carry your new way of thinking into other aspects of your life, you will become a better boss, coworker, spouse, parent, friend, etc...

The Platinum Rule for Sales Mastery is not only a better way to sell... *it's a better way to live!*

In the recently published book, *Why Don't Students Like School,* author Daniel Willingham, a cognitive psychologist, shares many insights with educators regarding the research on how the mind works and what it means for the classroom. One of the cognitive principles Willingham shares with educators that can be applied to help you remember what you read about sales mastery in this book is that, "memory is a residue of thought." In other words, memory is not a function of what someone wants to remember; it is a product of what one thinks about. In an effort to help you remember what you have read in this book, we have added reflection questions at various points in this second edition of the Sales Mastery book. The reason for doing so is that when reading a book such as this one the information is held in working memory to help make sense of what is being read. Unless you stop and take the time to think about what you have been reading the information that was read will not move from working memory to long-term memory and surely be forgotten. You have no doubt experienced this principle in action when reading other books. At the time, you were totally in sync with what it was you were reading and able to follow along with the story line or information being presented by the author—just like you are doing now—but then sadly unable to remember the details of what you had read later when telling a friend about it. You probably shook your head in disbelief when realizing you were not able to recall the details of what you read even though you were "really into the book" while in the act of reading it. There is no cause for alarm; the reason you could not recall the information was that you did not take the time to think about what you were reading so you naturally forgot it due to the cognitive principle that "memory is a residue of thought.

To assist the reader in remembering behavioral styles and how they apply to sales mastery, you will note this symbol "❓" at various points in the book. When you see the symbol we encourage you to take the time to stop and think of the answers to the reflection questions posed to store what you had read to that point in long-term memory. In doing so, you will be able to recall what you had read and apply it later to your life or daily activities as a sales professional.

SECTION I

the four
behavioral styles

F or some of you, the "4 styles" model of human behavior is a
new concept. However, many of you have probably run across
this concept on more than one occasion. "Behavioral styles,"
"personality types" and "temperament types" are not new, and
they all have validity.

People have been fascinated with studying behavioral styles for
thousands of years. Starting with the early astrologers, theorists have
sought to identify these behavioral styles. In ancient Greece, for
example, the physician Hippocrates outlined four temperaments:
Sanguine, Phlegmatic, Melancholic, and Choleric... more than four
decades before the birth of Christ. In 1921, famed psychologist Carl
Jung (the first to study personal styles scientifically) labeled people as
Intuitors, Thinkers, Feelers, and Sensors. Since then, psychologists have
produced more than a dozen models of behavioral differences, some
with sixteen or more possible behavioral blends. Sometimes the styles
have been given abstract behavioral-science names. In addition, some
teachers have drawn metaphors (as teaching aids) to birds, animals, or
even colors. Nevertheless, a common thread throughout the centuries is
the groupings of human behavior... in four categories.

Many of the concepts discussed in Section I of this book are based upon the proven concepts described in Dr. Alessandra's and Dr. O'Connor's books, "PeopleSmart" and "The Platinum Rule."

We will now introduce you to the four **_behavioral_** styles that are used throughout this book: the Director, Socializer, Thinker and Relater. As you read the description of each style, try to visualize previous or current customers who possess each style. Also ask yourself whether you would have been a more successful salesperson (or a co-worker, parent, spouse, or neighbor) had you adapted your behavior to match the style of past customers... regardless of whether they bought from you or not.

Note: *The Platinum Rule* is based upon observable behaviors, NOT "personalities" or "temperaments." This distinction is critical because human beings may change their behavior in the middle of a conversation. When you learn to adapt to the behavior that you are witnessing, you will stay in rapport with that person. People's personalities are deeply ingrained and slow to change, but behaviors can change in the blink of an eye. The way a person is acting at each moment in time will dictate how you should be selling to them.

1

directors...
the great intiators

⟵—————⟶

Directors initiate change, momentum and growth. They focus on attaining their goals, and their key need is to achieve their bottom-line results. The driving need for results, combined with their motto of "Lead, follow, or get out of the way," explains their no-nonsense, direct approach to getting things accomplished.

Directors are driven by an inner need to be in personal control. They want to take charge of situations so they can be sure of attaining their goals.

DIRECTORS NEED ACHIEVEMENT AND CONTROL

Directors want to win, so they may naturally challenge people or practices in the process. They accept challenges, take authority and plunge headfirst into solving problems. They tend to focus on administrative and operational controls and can work quickly and impressively by themselves.

Directors are naturals at being in control. They tend to be independent, strong-willed, precise, goal-oriented, and competitive with others... especially in a business environment. They try to shape their environment in order to overcome obstacles en route to their accomplishments. They demand freedom to manage themselves and others, and use their drive to come on top to become winners.

Directors like to get things done and make things happen. They start, juggle and maintain many projects concurrently. They may continue to add projects to their juggling routine until they are overloaded and then drop everything. They call this a "re-evaluation of their priorities." After reducing their workload, and stress levels, they often immediately start the whole process over again. Their motivation pattern contributes to a Director's tendency to be a "workaholic."

Their primary skills are their ability to get things done, lead others and make decisions. Directors have the ability to focus on one task... at the exclusion of everything else. They can block out doorbells, sirens, or other people while channeling all their energies into the specific job at hand.

ON THE OTHER HAND...

With each of the four behavioral styles, negative traits may accompany many of the positive attributes. Any characteristic, when taken to an extreme, has a shadow side.

For the Director, some negative traits may include stubbornness, impatience and an appearance of toughness. Directors tend to take control of other people and can have a low tolerance for the feelings, attitudes and shortcomings among co-workers and subordinates. Directors may annoy others because their constant need to come out on top can be offensive. With the Director, there are not "nine ways to skin a cat," there is only *one way*... the one preferred by the Director!

Directors like to move at a fast pace and tend to become impatient with delays. It is not unusual for a Director to call someone and launch into a conversation without saying "Hello." Oftentimes, Directors tend to view others who move at a slower speed as less competent.

Their weaknesses tend to include impatience, intolerance, poor listening habits and insensitivity to the needs of others. Their complete focus on their own goals and immediate tasks may make them appear aloof and uncaring.

One other thing to remember about Directors is that they will hold you to the terms and agreement of the sale. However, the same rules may not apply to them, because if the terms and agreement of the sale become inconvenient to them, they will lobby hard for you to bend the rules to accommodate their needs. If this happens, offer concessions sparingly (giving in will be seen as weakness) and be prepared to defend your decision to stick to the original agreement. Whenever you give a concession to a Director, get one in return – concession for concession. You might offer to negotiate new terms and agreements on future sales. Earning respect with Directors is critical to a long-term relationship.

DIRECTORS ARE DECISIVE

Directors embrace challenges, take authority, make decisions quickly, and expect others to do the same. They prefer to work with people who are decisive, efficient, receptive, competent and intelligent.

You may often find Directors in top management positions, and their personal strengths often contribute to their success in jobs such as a hard-driving reporter, a stockbroker, an independent consultant ... or a drill sergeant! Under pressure, Directors often get rid of their anger by ranting, raving or challenging others. While relieving their own inner tensions, they often create stress and tension within others.

"WINNING ISN'T EVERYTHING..."

The competitive nature of the Director is captured by Vince Lombardi's now-famous statement that, "Winning isn't everything... it's the only thing!" Directors can be so single-minded that they forget to take the time to "stop and smell the roses." If they do remember, they may return and comment, "I smelled twelve roses today ... how many did you smell?"

THE SOCIAL SCENE WITH DIRECTORS

Directors tend to take charge in social settings... sometimes inappropriately. Their relationships would improve if they would demonstrate their respect for other people's rights and opinions, allowing others to take charge… while "letting go." Directors have trouble having fun for fun's sake and usually have a specific purpose in mind. The competitive Director has a tendency to try to win even in relaxed social settings. He is always conscious of his standing in the "biggest and best" games. "Who has the biggest house?" "Who gives the best parties?" "Who plays the best golf?"

Directors often intertwine business and friendships. They like to mix their own business interests with pleasure, so they often pick friends from their work pool. Friendships often hinge on how much the friend agrees with the Director and helps him achieve his goals. Potential friendships are like an experiment with the Director: If it works, fine. If not, goodbye!

Director humor can be biting, often directed at others. Directors tend to take themselves too seriously and could benefit from learning to relax, laugh more and enjoying the lighter side of their own – and others' – actions.

Typical social behaviors of the Director may include:
- Competing actively in almost everything
- Participating in games or contests to win
- Wanting to know the purpose of a function
- Talking shop at gatherings
- Choosing friends by experimentation

Preferred social situations for a Director:
- Having many options from which to choose, for example: either jogging, attending an event, dining out, or playing cards
- Paying more attention to tactile things; less to emotions
- Doing only what they prefer to do
- Occasions that favor direct humor with an opportunity to demonstrate their talents
- Having a group subject to their control

- Being in charge of something at social events and activities: judging, giving directions, chairing a fund-raiser

THE DIRECTOR STYLE AT WORK

The Director can be an excellent problem solver and leader. Higher power positions and/or career areas motivate them (situations where they can take charge).

You will often find Directors in the following types of positions:

- President, CEO, or the formally recognized leader
- Politician
- Law enforcement officer
- Military officer
- Executive
- Manager
- Entrepreneur
- General contractor
- Coach

A typical Director sees himself as a solutions-oriented manager who enjoys a challenge just "because it's there." He likes the opportunity to complete tasks in a creative manner. He is generally viewed as having a high level of confidence, even when it isn't actually the case. The Director is often the first person to arrive in the morning and the last person to leave in the evening. At the extreme, their high results orientation can lead to an overextended work pattern and result in neglect for their personal and social lives.

Directors are often the first person at work to have a new efficiency "toy." They were the first to have a computer, a fax, mobile phone and (of course) a PDA. Saving time is always a priority for Directors so they can accomplish more.

Directors gain energy by taking risks. They do not feel as bound by conventional restrictions as other types and often feel free to bend rules that get in the way of results. They seek opportunities for change (or they create them!) just to satisfy their need for results. They may even gravitate toward high-risk situations because the excitement of the challenge fuels their drive to exert control in new areas or ways.

Directors realize that results can be gained through teamwork (and may actually develop a management approach that demands and supports teamwork), but it requires adaptation. The nature of the Director is to focus on his own individual actions and accomplishments. In his biography, Lee Iacocca, former CEO of Chrysler Corporation (a "Director legend"), discusses how he learned to merge his temperament with other styles as he finally arrived at the following management philosophy: "In the end, all business operations can be reduced to three words: people, products, profits. People come first. Unless you have a good team, you can't do much with the other two." Iacocca knew that good people were the means to an end.

Director business characteristics include:

- Prefers controlled time-frames
- Seeks personal control
- Gets to the point quickly
- Strives to feel important and be noteworthy in their jobs
- Demonstrates persistence and single-mindedness in reaching goals
- Expresses high ego need
- Prefers to downplay feelings and relationships
- Focuses on task actions that lead to achieving tangible outcomes
- Implements changes in the workplace
- Tends to freely delegate duties, enabling them to take on more tasks and pursue more goals

The preferred business situations for Directors:

- Calling the shots and telling others what to do
- Challenging workloads to fuel their energy levels
- Personally overseeing, or at least knowing about, their employees' or co-workers' business activities

- Saying what's on their minds without being concerned about hurting anybody's feelings
- Taking risks and being involved in facilitating changes
- Interpreting the rules and answering to themselves alone
- Interested in the answers to "what" questions
- Seeing a logical road toward advancement of achieving goals

THE DIRECTOR SALESPERSON

If you are (or someone you know) is a Director salesperson, the natural tendency is to launch rather quickly into a sales presentation. You get right to the point by telling your prospect the bottom-line benefit of using your product to provide a solution. Your natural tendency is to spend little time on chitchat or getting to know your prospects... unless it's required to get the sale! Directors move quickly, and if a prospect does not see the benefit of your proposal, you move on to the next prospect.

Directors have a fast, efficient manner and total focus on goals that make them more comfortable than most people with cold calling. They are able to tolerate negatives as a necessary part of the sales process. Their bottom-line orientation fits their focus on products or services, which adds efficiency to their customer acquisition processes. Directors tend to sell by painting a convincing picture of the benefits of their product or service.

Their best "fit" is with standard products or services where a match can be determined. Products or services requiring lengthy tailoring, customization and/or development (such as complex computer, communication or consultation systems) try their patience. Directors prefer sales processes where quick decisions can be made based on rational, concrete, reality-based data. Directors often like working with products that fill a recognized need rather than in areas where expectations and opportunities have to be developed in conjunction with each customer.

Director salespeople are very careful about time... especially their own! They tend to make specific time appointments and arrive punctually. They are clear about their desired results from customer contacts and quickly present the features and benefits offered by their product or service.

THE DIRECTOR CUSTOMER

The Director customer will make decisions relatively quickly when presented with factual information. He wants to see the bottom-line impact of the product (or service) solution and wants you to provide enough detail (but not too much!) so that he judges you as competent to handle his business. Directors generally are businesslike, straightforward and to-the-point; they prefer others to be the same. They expect people to take their goals and concerns seriously and offer them solutions. They respect salespeople who look and act in a professional manner. Also, they expect the salesperson to deliver the results they promised.

What this customer wants to know is how your product or service will solve his problems most effectively right now. The Director is not a natural listener, so details and lengthy explanations are likely to be lost on him. The salesperson is expected to provide immediately useful information and recommendations that will move the Director toward his goals. Director customers will often ask detailed questions more as a test of the salesperson's credibility than because he wants to know the answers. If it is necessary to provide detailed information to a Director, it should be done in writing so the Director can review it later.

Director customers look for product solutions that will help them achieve their goals. They maintain control of the sales process and prefer salespeople who provide the information and data necessary to make a sound decision. They are competitive and respond well to products or services that are "the best."

Directors expect results now and are impatient with waiting. They expect salespeople to respond to impossible deadlines even if it means sacrificing personal time. They aren't especially interested in developing relationships with the salesperson, but it is important for them to believe that the salesperson can help them get their results. They like being recognized for their achievements, and respond well to awards banquets, "special customer" celebrations and other recognitions of their involvement with the buying/owning process.

Time is an important factor for the goal-oriented Director. He does not tolerate having salespeople waste his time and he does not want to waste theirs. This includes time spent on "unimportant" chitchat. Directors are more comfortable as team leaders than as team players. Because of this, they tend to make decisions themselves rather than getting others involved.

Directors like to have choices. They like to have options and exercise their decision-making power. Each possibility should be a reasonable choice backed by evidence supporting its probability of success. This type of buyer has clear objectives to achieve and responds to those who can demonstrate that their product or service can efficiently achieve results.

DIRECTORS AT A GLANCE:

- Need to be in charge; dislike inaction
- Act quickly and decisively
- Think practically... not theoretically or hypothetically
- Want highlighted facts
- Strive for results
- Need personal freedom to manage self and others
- Like changes and new opportunities
- Prefer to delegate details
- Cool, independent and competitive
- Have a low tolerance for feelings, attitudes or advice of others
- Work quickly and impressively by themselves
- Want to be recognized for their accomplishments
- Easily stimulated to engage in arguments and conflict
- Interested in administrative controls

Based on what you have just read about the Director, can you think of a friend, family member, or co-worker that has this behavioral style? Perhaps it is a neighbor, sibling, or boss. What behaviors does that person exhibit to make you think he or she is a Director? Does that person work in a position or career that is consistent with those typically held by Directors? If this person were to become a customer of yours, do you recall two or three things that you read that could increase the odds of him or her buying something from you?

Please note that if for some reason you do not remember the answers to the set of questions posed above, it is well worth the effort to turn back and find the answers to the questions in order to remember what you have read and use it later to perfect your sales mastery skills. Please do the same for those questions that are sure to follow later in the book to remember what you read.

2

socializers...
the great talkers

$$\longleftrightarrow$$

Socializers are the great talkers because they are friendly, enthusiastic and like to be where the action is. They thrive on admiration, acknowledgement, compliments and applause. They want to have fun and enjoy life. Energetic and fast-paced, Socializers tend to place more priority on relationships than on tasks. They influence others by their optimistic, friendly demeanor and they focus primarily on attaining positive approval from others.

SOCIALIZERS NEED ATTENTION AND APPROVAL

Admiration and acceptance are extremely important to Socializers. Often, they are not as concerned about winning or losing as how they look while they're "playing the game." The Socializer's greatest fear is public humiliation: appearing uninvolved, unattractive, unsuccessful or unacceptable to others. These frightening forms of social rejection threaten the Socializer's core need for approval. As a result, when conflict occurs, Socializers may abruptly take flight for more favorable environments.

The Socializers' primary strengths are their enthusiasm, persuasiveness and friendliness. They are "idea-a-minute" people who have the ability to get others caught up in their dreams. With great persuasion, they shape their environments by building personal alliances to accomplish their results. Then they seek nods and comments of approval and recognition for those results. If compliments do not come, Socializers may invent their own! They are stimulating, talkative and communicative.

Socializers are generally open with their ideas and feelings, but sometimes only at superficial levels. They are not as prone to "wearing their hearts on their sleeves" as Relaters, but will happily share their thoughts and ideas about almost any topic at any given time. They are animated, interactive storytellers who have no qualms about "creative exaggeration." They love an audience and thrive on involvement with people. They tend to work quickly and enthusiastically with others. They are risk takers and base many of their actions and decisions on natural impulse and feelings. Their greatest irritations are doing repetitive or complex tasks, being alone, or not having access to a telephone!

ON THE OTHER HAND...

Their weaknesses are too much involvement in too many projects, impatience, aversion to being alone, and short attention spans. They become bored quickly and easily. When a little data comes in, Socializers tend to make sweeping generalizations. They may not thoroughly investigate; assuming someone else will do it, or they may procrastinate because re-doing something just isn't exciting enough. When Socializers feel they do not have enough stimulation and involvement, they get bored and look for something new... repeatedly.

When taken to an extreme, Socializer behaviors may appear superficial, haphazard, erratic and overly emotional. Their need for acknowledgement can lead to self-absorption. They have a casual approach to time and often drive the other styles "crazy" with their missed deadlines and lateness. The fun loving, life-of-the-party Socializer can be undisciplined, forgetful, overly talkative, and too eager for credit and recognition. Their natural humor often bubbles over even in serious situations, which should have called for more reserved behavior.

Socializers are often found in positions such as sales, public relations specialists, talk show hosts, trial attorneys, social directors on cruise ships, hotel personnel and other people-intensive, high-visibility careers. Audience reactions stimulate them and they thrive in entertainment fields where their natural, animated actions can flow easily. They like to charm friends, co-workers and audiences with their friendliness and enthusiasm.

You probably know some Socializers in your family, at the office, or at home. They are the ones who always have something to say. They are the people you ask, "How is it going," and twenty minutes later, they are still talking your ear off. The thing they love to talk about the most is one thing in particular... themselves.

THE SOCIAL SCENE WITH THE SOCIALIZER

Socializers love people and specialize in socializing. Most aspects of their lives are open books and they are likely to discuss most subjects, no matter how close or distant your relationship. Showing and sharing their feelings come naturally to this behavioral type. Of the four styles, Socializers are the most comfortable talking about personal topics: marriage, finances, politics, aspirations and problems. They jump from topic to topic and activity to activity, often leaving their listeners bewildered.

Socializers revel in humor (even if directed at themselves) and often tell hair-raising anecdotes about their experiences. The wilder the situation the better... and a little embellishment only make their stories sound that much more exciting and entertaining. They view this tendency toward stretching the facts as spicing things up to be more interesting to the listener. They love to talk; telling a story better and funnier than it actually happened comes naturally to them.

This tendency to talk and tell stories can be a problem when privacy or confidences are involved. A Socializer naturally considers all conversations to be an open book, and unless they're expressly told not to tell anyone about the topic, they are not likely to realize the importance of keeping confidences.

Socializers are naturally optimistic and ready with an encouraging pep talk when the people around them are down or have problems. They praise and support others, in part, in order to create a positive environment where they can satisfy their own needs for social approval. Compliments and encouragement make them feel good, even when the praise is directed at someone else!

Socializers like to be the life of the party. You will often find them in the middle of a circle of admirers. Their willingness to discuss any topic often invites controversy and they love a lively debate. They gain energy from the dynamics of relationships and talking; they despise feeling bored. People rally around them because they know how to create fun and find (or make) the action. They are playful and enjoy companionship; they hate isolation.

Of the four types, Socializers most want to be liked by others. They will monitor the body language, vocal inflections, and eye contact of others to make sure they are being viewed in a favorable light. Should they detect that they have fallen out of favor among those they are entertaining, they will work even harder to win back the good graces of others. It hurts their feelings when disliked by others; even the slightest criticism can be deflating.

Socializers love being the first on the block to have a new "toy"... especially if it has lots of bells, whistles, and lights! Their involvement with gadgets is a form of fun as well as a way to simplify their workload. Additionally, showing off their new toy gives them more opportunities to promote and persuade.

Socializers are notorious for being "fashionably late." People may think they are trying to make a grand entrance, but often their being late generally results from their casual approach (and resulting miscalculations) to time. They often forget details of social obligations and get so caught up in what they are presently doing that they lose track of time and place.

Typical social behavior of the Socializer includes:

- Wants to be liked and admired
- Fears public humiliation

- Discusses most subjects, regardless of how distant or casual the relationship
- Naturally warm, expressive and enthusiastic
- Enjoys bouncing ideas off others
- Reluctant to fight or confront stressful people or situations
- Perceives life according to feelings
- Naturally discusses emotions with others
- Chooses associates and friends by "gut instinct" and trial-and-error

Preferred social situations of the Socializer:

- Events and activities involving personal interaction and contact
- Hosting or attending impromptu gatherings
- Being with fun people with different interests
- Seeks more positive people and settings
- Finds it easy to laugh, joke and play games
- Often seeks high-visibility positions: host, storyteller, emcee, etc...
- Prefers humor that pokes fun at foibles... their own and others'
- Tries to diffuse mild tension with jokes or funny observations
- Prefers to ignore sources of stress (such as conflict or complex tasks)
- Likes to share the moment with others

THE SOCIALIZER'S STYLE AT WORK

Socializers prefer careers that maximize their influence and persuasion with other people. They tend to gravitate to environments that allow them to socialize, mingle, and gain positive feedback.

Socializers often work in these types of careers:

- Customer relations
- Public relations
- Entertainment: acting, singing, reporting, public speaking... being on stage or in the public eye
- Professional host or emcee (talk show, party, restaurant, airline, etc...)
- Recreational director

- Politician
- Salesperson
- Teacher

Socializers are happy working with other people. They like being treated with warmth, friendliness, and approval. Because they favor interacting with people on more than just a business level, they want to be your friend before doing business with you.

The Socializer likes a quick pace and often moves about the office in a flurry of activity. He even walks in a way that reflects his optimism and pace ... lively and energetically. He tends to think aloud and often walks around the office talking to almost everyone. While this may appear to be "goofing off" to more Director-style managers, Socializers pick up much of their information by talking to others and observing their surroundings. They are likely to brainstorm about matters with virtually everyone they encounter. It's important for them to find out how other people feel about their ideas. They also like feedback and occasional pats on the back that these impromptu encounters provide. They enjoy a casual, relaxed environment where their impulses can have free rein. Desk hopping also satisfies their need for companionship. They like to play and mingle as they learn, earn and do practically everything else.

Since Socializers are naturally talkative and people-oriented, dealing with people who are in positions of power meet their need for inclusion by others, popularity, social recognition and relative freedom from a lot of detail. Socializers are good at getting others caught up in their ideas. Their persuasive powers may simultaneously amaze admirers and frustrate detractors. These smooth-talking tendencies can (at their extreme), be perceived as silver-tongued oration or evasive double-talk. The Socializer may appear to be a verbal Pied Piper or even a wheeling and dealing con artist.

Socializers want companionship and social recognition, so their contributions to group morale often satisfy those needs. They encourage their employees, peers, and superiors to excel. They typically look outside themselves to renew their energies and enjoy motivational books, tapes and speeches. They need these pick-me-ups to recharge their batteries and help them overcome obstacles. Their typically optimistic outlook changes problems into challenges or opportunities.

The Big Picture is much more interesting to Socializers than supporting details. After seeing the broad overview, they prefer not to personally dwell on specifics. Their enthusiasm helps them generate many ideas and their tendency to get feedback from everyone around them helps select ideas that have a good chance to succeed.

The Socializer's tendency to talk more than the other styles sometimes gets them in trouble by saying inappropriate things. They are naturally impulsive; sometimes their spontaneous behavior is energizing, but sometimes it is frustrating. They continually seek out new ideas. Sometimes this is irritating to the people around them who think that a solution has been settled upon... only to have the Socializer start off on a new round of potential solutions. While others think the Socializer was committed to something, the Socializer just thought he was thinking aloud. Socializers are much better at generating ideas than implementing them.

Socializers do not respond well to authoritative or dictatorial management styles, often possessed and displayed by the Director, especially under stress or tight deadlines. The boss that orders the Socializer to do one thing may receive just the opposite. The Socializer may get defensive and become less willing to cooperate. On the other hand, the boss that chooses to take the time to inspire the Socializer to accomplish something, will find it hard to find a more dedicated, committed, hard worker. This is particularly true once the Socializer has had time to "connect" the significance of the work to their dreams, their financial future, or sees it as a chance to "shine" in front of management or a client.

Socializers' business characteristics include:

- Likes to brainstorm and interact with colleagues and others
- Wants freedom from control, details, or complexity
- Likes to have the chance to influence, persuade or motivate others
- Likes the feeling of being a key part of an exciting team

- Wants to be included by others in important projects, activities or events
- Gets easily bored by routine and repetition
- May trust others without reservation; takes others at their word and does not check for themselves
- Typically have short attention spans, so they do better with frequent, short breaks
- Prefer talking to listening

Preferred business situations for Socializers include:

- Likes to work interactively with others
- Needs personal feedback and discussion to get – or stay – on course
- Likes to mingle with all levels of associates and calls them by their first names
- Enjoys compliments about themselves and their accomplishments
- Seeks stimulating environments that are friendly and favorable
- Motivated to work toward known, specific, quickly attainable incentives or external motivators (dislikes pursuits which drag out over long time periods)
- Open to verbal or demonstrated guidance for transferring ideas into action
- Likes to start projects, but prefers to let others handle the follow-through and detail work

THE SOCIALIZER SALESPERSON

The Socializer salesperson has a positive attitude, is enthusiastic, optimistic and has a natural orientation toward people. These attributes provide them with a head start in the sales process. Socializers are excellent at making contact, networking and socializing. They tend to get bored easily. Their best sales situation is one that gives them an opportunity to meet and greet a lot of people, but does not require a lengthy needs analysis or negotiation process. Examples of products that fit this natural style are real estate, cars, office equipment and club membership sales.

Socializer salespeople like situations that give them a lot of freedom and provide variety and fun. The Socializer salesperson puts special emphasis on appearance and looking prosperous and successful. The Socializer tends to have the newest cell phone, stylish clothes, and other symbols that say, "Hey, look at me!"

They excel when the product or service they are selling brings happiness to their customers. They especially like to be involved with products or services that help their customers look good: clothes, beauty services, jewelry and status symbols such as fine art, yachts, or private airplanes.

With their creative minds and advanced communication skills, they are great at painting mental pictures for customers. They may use sentences that being with, "Just imagine yourself…" or "You'll be the envy of your neighbors when…" They tend to be the best of the four styles for generating a long list of corresponding benefits for every feature offered by a product or service they are selling.

The Socializer salesperson is an oddity in some respects. Although they will take the time to know the customers' personal likes and dislikes, as well as readily share their own, they may forget their names, birthdays, the college they attended, and so forth. This is not because they don't care, (they have every intention of remembering and doing all these things) but once they move on to the next person they often forget the intimate details of the previous customer to better focus on the opportunity at hand.

Using customer contact software is a terrific idea for helping Socializer salespeople leveraging any short-term knowledge about each new relationship.

THE SOCIALIZER CUSTOMER

The Socializer customer will make purchasing decisions quickly if they become excited by an opportunity placed before them. They dislike being bogged down with a lot of details and data about the features of the product or service, but will listen intently to the benefits. In fact, with their fast, creative minds, they often see the benefits before you can point them out.

When this happens, compliment them for their quick thinking and their "big picture" vision, but otherwise… don't speak! At that moment, you are the second-best salesperson in the conversation… they will sell themselves.

Socializers base many of their decisions on intuition or first impressions. They need to be liked and admired; it helps if salespeople understand what makes them look good… both personally and professionally. They look for fun and creativity in the buying/selling process and respond well to invitations to social gatherings: lunches, golf outings, celebrations, etc. They prefer to know salespeople personally, and they want the salesperson to know their likes and dislikes.

Socializers do not like bureaucracy and paperwork. They want the sales process to be simple and easy… they want to say "yes" and then have everything magically happen without their further involvement. They are so positive and optimistic that they often expect more than the salesperson intended to deliver.

Socializers prefer to work with people in a dynamic and creative environment. They are "big picture" people who enjoy having many possibilities, but may then need help from the salesperson to narrow the choices and focus on one solution. Once a decision is made, they tend to be very enthusiastic and may help sell the solution to other people or departments within the company.

Socializers will go with a risky decision or a new product if they are convinced that it will help move them closer to their dream. It is also important for them to know there is not a steep learning curve to using a product or service. If they suspect so, they may decide against the purchase. As such, they expect the salesperson to be part of their "team" to help them get them through the learning curve quickly.

SOCIALIZERS AT A GLANCE:
- Craves interaction and human contact
- Enthusiastic, expressive and lively actions
- Spontaneous actions and decisions
- Concerned with approval and appearances

- Emotion-based decision makers
- "Big picture" thinkers who get bored with details
- Likes changes and innovations
- Needs help getting and staying organized
- Dislikes conflict
- Maintains a positive, optimistic orientation to life
- Exaggerates and generalizes
- Tends to dream aloud and gets others caught up in their dreams
- Jumps from one activity to another
- Works quickly and excitedly with others
- Seeks acknowledgement from others
- Likes to exercise their persuasive skills

Do you know someone that loves to be around other people and tends to be talkative and entertaining? Perhaps that person is a Socializer. Based on what you just read what other behaviors does that person exhibit to make you think he or she is a Socializer? Do you remember the things that Socializers want most out of the sales process to increase the likelihood that they will buy from as a customer?

3

thinkers...
the great analyzers

Thinkers are analytical, persistent and systematic problem solvers. They are more concerned with logic and content than style. Thinkers prefer involvement with products and services under specific, controlled, predictable conditions so they can continue to perfect the performance, process, and results.

THINKERS SEEK ORDER AND ASSURANCES

The primary concern of the Thinker is accuracy; this often means that emotions take a back seat. They believe feelings are more subjective and distort objectivity. Their biggest fear is of uncontrolled emotions and irrational acts, which might prevent the achievement of their objectives. They are uncomfortable with emotionality and/or irrationality in others. Thinkers strive to avoid embarrassment by attempting to control both themselves and their emotions. Of the four styles, Thinkers are the most risk-conscious and have a high need for accuracy. Combining these factors may lead them to an over-reliance on the collection of information and input from too many sources.

Thinkers prefer to deal with tasks rather than people and they like to have clearly defined priorities. They like to operate at a methodical pace, which also allows them to check and recheck their work. They tend to focus on the serious, more complicated sides of situations but, when they are relaxed, their natural mental wit does enable them to appreciate the lighter side of things. They are often the first to see the bizarre nature or potential in situations.

Of the four styles, Thinkers are the most cerebrally oriented. They make decisions logically and cautiously to increase the probability that they take the best available action. They are deliberate and strive to be technically perfect. Thinkers demand a lot from themselves (and others) and may succumb to overly critical tendencies. Generally, they tend to keep their criticisms to themselves, hesitating to tell people what they think is deficient or incorrect. They typically share information, both positive and negative, only if requested, or on a need-to-know basis... and only if they have received assurances that there will be no negative consequences to them.

When Thinkers have definite, precise knowledge of facts and conditions, they quietly hold their ground. They can be indirectly assertive when they perceive they are in control of a relationship or their environment. After determining the specific risks, margins of error, and any other variables that significantly influence the desired results, they will take action. Often times, their action may be subtle and indirect. However, if they can control the outcomes, their actions may be more swift and direct.

Strengths of the Thinker include accuracy, independence, clarification and verification, fine-tuning and organization. They naturally focus on expectations (e.g.: policies, practices, and procedures), processes and outcomes. They want to know how things work so their own actions can be correct. Their core personal need is for autonomy in controlling the processes involved in fulfilling expectations in moving toward the intended outcomes.

Thinkers tend to be serious and orderly and are likely to be perfectionists. They tend to focus on the more critical details in the process of work and become irritated by surprises or glitches. They like organization, structure, and dislike involvement either with too many people or with any one person for too long a period. They work meticulously by themselves and prefer objective, task-oriented, intellectual work environments. Thinkers remain disciplined with their own use of time and are most comfortable under controlled circumstances. They can be skeptical and even become cynical. They like to see things in writing as a way of measuring or validating expectations and feedback from others.

ON THE OTHER HAND...

Because Thinkers like to be right, they prefer checking processes themselves. This tendency toward perfectionism, when taken to an extreme, can result in "analysis paralysis." These overly cautious traits may result in worry that the process is not progressing exactly right, which further promotes their tendency to behave in a critical, detached way.

Thinkers may appear to be aloof, meticulous and critical. Their fear of being wrong can make them over-reliant on the collection of information and slow to reach a decision. While Thinkers are natural observers who ask many questions, they may focus too much on downside possibilities and remote dangers... at the expense of missing up-side opportunities and bottom-line payoffs.

In their effort to avoid conflict, Thinkers often refrain from voluntarily expressing their inner thoughts and feelings. This lack of direct feedback may lead to future misunderstandings and weaken relationship-building opportunities.

THE DEEP THINKER

Perhaps you live or work with someone who is quiet, individualistic, slow to speak or show emotion, and covets his or her privacy. Oftentimes, there is a lot going on inside their head as they agonize over what to do next, how their feelings operate, and ultimately, the process of doing the right thing. They tend to put their emotions under a microscope then analyze and reanalyze them to make sure their response was proper given the stimulus that set them off.

ON THE SOCIAL SCENE WITH THE THINKER

The Thinker is a contemplator, examining the pros and cons of any given situation and trying to consider everything. Their need to weigh possibilities and ramifications can cause stress for other (more impetuous) behavioral types, and sometimes Thinkers contemplate a situation until the opportunity slips away completely. However, the Thinker's innate caution can serve to offset the more impetuous ideas or decisions made by of some other types.

Thinkers are astute observers of their surroundings. They absorb virtually everything around them, taking in and processing information about people and things. Many Thinkers report having difficulty falling asleep or getting back to sleep if they wake up during the night because they can't turn off everything that is running through their minds. Thinkers fascinate themselves by processing many of the complexities of life (that often escapes the other types).

Thinkers typically act reserved and distant until they feel they know you well enough to let down their guard; building trust with them often takes time. They plan and select their relationships cautiously. Because they are such private people, they sometimes seem mysterious or even conniving.

Unlike Socializers, Thinkers do not prefer team sports or group recreational pursuits. Being more on the introverted side, they like to engage in independent indoor and outdoor recreational activities. In the outdoors, you may find them bird watching, kayaking, hiking, camping, fishing, etc. Indoor activities may include stamp collecting, painting, music, computer games, board games, model building, woodworking, etc. Regardless of the activity, Thinkers often become experts in their hobby or endeavor. Indeed, the one way to get a Thinker to have a conversation is to ask about his or her hobby or recreational pursuit. You may discover that you will learn much more about the subject than you may have ever wanted to know.

Since Thinkers do not readily discuss their feelings or often even their thoughts, their non-verbal responses can speak volumes about how they really think or feel. That first little smirk or quick, one-syllable laugh can tell you that they are pleased. Watch the Thinkers' body language for indicators of how they feel about someone or something.

Thinkers are not comfortable telling stories or anecdotes about themselves. When pressed for an opinion or reaction, they may sidestep the issue completely. Being asked to "talk about their feelings" is a request that strikes fear in the heart of the Thinker, because they are not comfortable doing it.

Thinker humor typically shows a down-home, dry, witty perspective, often from an unexpected angle. Perhaps you have seen those comics that deliver the jokes in a deadpan manner; they do not "act funny," but what they say is clever, witty, and point to life's ironies... Bob Newhart and Steven Wright come to mind. Even though they do not express feelings and thoughts easily, they often capture them with timeless stories that contain penetrating insights about human nature.

Small groups of people are much more comfortable for the Thinker since it takes them time to establish a comfort zone with others. They are fearful of mistakes or criticisms and interact with people who pose no threat to them.

Typical social behavior of the Thinker includes:

- Quiet and observant; likes to collect information before entering a relationship
- Socially cool and distant; waits for other to take the initiative
- Discreet and tactful; not likely to tell secrets or the naked truth
- Serious; suspicious of others unless they have previously proven themselves
- Guarded; prefers a small group of friends and work associates

Preferred social situations of the Thinker include:

- Attending a planned, private small gathering of close friends who have consistently proven to be trustworthy in the past
- Participating in organized activities where they can demonstrate (and be appreciated for) their expertise

- Conversing logically about areas of personal knowledge, adding key input to the conversation
- Talking, and listening to, ideas and facts, not feelings
- Conflict-free environments which prize individuality

The Thinker's style at work:

Thinkers prefer careers in which they can strive for perfection, creativity and completeness.

Thinkers often work in these types of positions:

- Forecasters (political, weather, etc...)
- Critics (film, history, literary, etc...)
- Engineers
- Research scientists
- Data analysts
- Accountants/auditors
- Artists/sculptors/architects
- Inventors
- College professors
- Veterinarians
- Technicians and mechanics

Thinkers see themselves as logical problem solvers who like structure, concentrate on key details and ask specific questions about critical factors. They are masters at following important, established directions and standards, while still meeting the need to control the process by their own actions. Process-oriented Thinkers want to know why something works, since such insight allows them to determine for themselves the most logical way to achieve the expected results... from themselves and others.

In business, Thinkers are the refiners of reality. They seek neither utopias nor quick fixes. Because of their risk-averse tendencies, they may overly plan when change becomes inevitable. Planning is their way of improving their odds. They like working in circumstances that promote quality in products or services. When possible, they prepare ahead of time for their projects and then work diligently to perfect them to the nth degree. Their thorough preparation minimizes the probability of errors. They prefer finishing tasks on schedule, but not if it might be at the expense of making a mistake. They dislike last minute rushing and inadequate checking or review.

Thinkers prefer logic and rely on reasoning to avoid mistakes. They tend to check, recheck, and check again. They may become mired down with accumulating facts and over-analysis. They are uncomfortable freely giving opinions or partial information until they have exhausted all their resources. This process can frustrate other behavioral types who want to know what is going on now.

Whether or not this type opts for a scientific or artistic career, Thinkers often follow a rational method or intuitive, logical progression to achieve their objectives. Because of their natural inclination to validate and improve upon accepted processes, Thinkers tend to generate the most native creativity of the four types. Consequently, they often explore new ways of viewing old questions, concerns and opportunities.

Thinkers seek solace and answers by focusing inwardly. Their natural orientation is toward objects and away from people. From their perspective, people are unpredictable and complicate matters. With more people added to the formula, the chances of getting unpredictable results increase. Thinkers choose to work with colleagues who promote objectivity and thoroughness in the office. When encouraged to do so, Thinkers can share their rich supplies of information with co-workers who can benefit from their wealth of experience and knowledge.

When discussions and tempers become hot and heavy, Thinkers may start looking for an exit... or at least a fallback position to reassess their strategy. They want peace and tranquility and tend to avoid and reject hostility and outward expressions of aggression. They can numb themselves to conflict to such an extent that they may have difficulty tapping into their feelings. They can become perfectionistic and worrisome, both with themselves and with others.

Business characteristics of the typical Thinker include:

- Concerned with process; wants to know how something works
- Intuitive and original; once they know the expected structure, they may invent their own structure, method, or model
- More interested in quality than quantity; prefer lower output to inferior results
- Wants to be right; employs logical thinking processes in order to avoid mistakes
- Sometimes impedes progress with their constant checking and rechecking
- Dislikes unplanned changes and surprises
- Rejects open aggression

Preferred business situations for the Thinker include:

- Colleagues and superiors who do not criticize work or ideas, especially in public
- Situations where they can set the quality control standards and check to see if they are properly implemented
- Working with complete information systems, or being empowered to formulate their own methods
- Superiors who value correctness and the Thinker's key role in the organization
- Organized and process-oriented workplaces with little emphasis on socializing

THE THINKER SALESPERSON

The natural style of the Thinker salesperson is to provide the prospect with lots of precise facts and logical information. Because Thinkers are not relationship oriented, they perform best in sales situations involving technical, faster moving products, where buying decisions are based primarily on technical capabilities. Thinkers work well with professional buyers, as they tend to give them an organized, logical presentation, without spending time on small talk.

Thinkers take the time to understand the needs of the customer, as well as the process in which the product or service is expected to perform. Their proposals tend to emphasize the technical features and superiority of their product or service. Thinkers try to provide a "bullet-proof" solution for their customers and are often surprised if the purchase decision is made on a basis that is not completely "rational."

Thinker salespeople are painstaking information gatherers, and they carefully piece together the needs of the customer and the requirements of the organization before presenting a solution. Their natural style is to depend on their ability to provide solutions rather than focusing on the interpersonal relationships. They prefer selling scenarios where they can analyze the situation, map out a solution, and then leave any training, installation or follow-up to someone else.

THE THINKER CUSTOMER

The Thinker customer is task-oriented and needs information and specific data to make his decision. Thinkers want to understand the process of the sale, as well as how the product or service will operate within their current systems. They need time to evaluate the data. They tend to respond positively to graphs and charts that visually clarify the information. All information presented to Thinkers should be well organized and logical.

Thinkers sometimes become lost in non-essential details (that they believe may have some hidden, less obvious significance). Helping them re-focus on the "big picture" and comparative benefits between competing choices can help them to accelerate their decisions.

Thinker customers respond well to efforts to reduce the buying risk. Guarantees, free trials and pilot programs can reduce obstacles to the Thinker's purchasing options. By comparison with the other styles, Thinkers also tend to be concerned about the impact of the purchase decision on the organization; how it fits into policies, procedures, and existing circumstances. Thinkers seldom make their decisions based on only relationships, but it is important that they respect and trust the salesperson and his organization to "make right" any problems encountered after the purchase.

Thinkers have subdued body language and verbal responses, making them hard to "read." If you stop to think about it (pardon the pun), the Thinker is the easiest style to identify because of their low-key, deliberate, measured and reserved behaviors. They are put off by a perceived excess of either directness or uninformed enthusiasm by salespeople and view too much intensity as distracting and unnecessary. The Thinker customer wants to know that the salesperson is knowledgeable in his field.

Thinkers prefer a minimum of interaction and would rather have a few short phone calls than an intensive series of meetings. Thinker customers tend to avoid personal involvement and are more comfortable with discrete or formal buying procedures.

THINKERS AT A GLANCE:
- Thinks logically and analytically
- Needs data and their questions answered
- Likes to be right, correct
- Likes organization and structure
- Asks many questions about specific details
- Prefers objective, task-oriented, intellectual work environment
- Needs to understand processes
- Are cautious decision makers
- Prefers to do things themselves
- Works slowly and precisely alone
- Likes to be admired for their accuracy
- Avoids conflict and over-involvement with others
- Likes to contemplate and reconsider
- Likes problem solving methods and approaches

Based on what you just read about the Thinker, do you know someone who has that behavioral style? Does that person have some of strengths that are unique to Thinkers? Does he or she hold any of the positions or careers that are tailor-made for the Thinker? What is it you read about the body language of the Thinker that impacts your ability to get them to do business with you?

4

relaters...
the great helpers

Relaters are warm, supportive and predictable. They are the most group-oriented of all of the four styles. Having friendly, lasting, first name relationships with others is one of their most important desires. They dislike interpersonal conflict so much that when they disagree, they will often keep silent. At other times, they may say what they think other people want to hear. They have natural counseling tendencies and are supportive of other people's feelings, ideas and goals. Other people usually feel comfortable interacting with Relaters because of their low-key, non-confrontational nature. Relaters are natural listeners and like to be part of networks of people who share common interests.

RELATERS NEED RESPECT AND TRANQUILITY

Relaters focus on getting acquainted and building trust. They are inwardly flustered by pushy, aggressive behavior. They are cooperative, steady workers who function well as team members. They strive to maintain stability and to create a peaceful environment for others. While "venturing into the unknown" may be an intriguing concept for some other types, Relaters prefer to stick with what they already know and have experienced. *Risk* is a dangerous word to Relaters. They may even stay in an unpleasant environment rather than take chances by making a change. Disruption in their routine patterns can cause them distress. When faced with a change, they need to think it through slowly, systematically and piece-by-piece in preparing for the change. Finding elements of sameness within those changes can help minimize their stress.

Relaters yearn for more tranquility and constancy in their lives than the other three types. They operate on an emotional plane that has occasional, moderate mood swings from melancholy to happy. They rarely have emotional highs like that of the Socializer, but the change is noticeable. This reflects their natural need for composure, stability and balance. Their relationships are generally amiable and their relaxed disposition makes them approachable and warm. They are easy-going, calm and operate at a deliberate, measured pace.

The primary strengths of Relaters are their accommodation, appreciation for – and patience with – others. They are courteous, friendly and willing to share responsibilities. They are good implementers who are persistent and will usually follow-through on the completion of action plan steps; they do so because they hate to let other people down or fear confrontation.

ON THE OTHER HAND. . .

Relaters have difficulty speaking up and expressing their true feelings, especially if it might create conflict. They appear to go along with others even when they inwardly do not agree. This tendency creates an environment where the more aggressive types may take advantage of the Relater. Their lack of assertiveness sometimes results in hurt feelings because they do not let others know how they truly feel. They can be overly sensitive and easily bullied.

Their need for harmony makes them slower at making decisions as they privately try to find solutions that most likely lead to consensus. People of other styles often view this behavior as being weak or indecisive. In fact, their slow but deliberate pace results from their desire to minimize risk in unknown situations, partially by inclusion of others in the decision making process. The Relater's need to stay personally involved in the detailed aspects of work often makes them hesitant to delegate effectively. They often would rather shoulder more work than inconvenience someone else by asking for help.

Relaters are often found in the helping professions such as: counseling, teaching, social work, ministry, psychology, nursing and human resource developments. Relaters are among the most patient and supportive parents.

THE SOCIAL SCENE WITH THE RELATER

Relaters are quiet, evenly paced and inwardly focused individuals. They recharge their batteries and renew their energy by looking for answers within themselves and a relatively small group of friends, family and associates. As warm and open as they may appear, they have private thoughts that they are reluctant to divulge. Their energy drains when called upon to share how they feel about private matters or controversial topics that may offend someone. They would rather sit back, observe other's feelings, and then offer a more measured response based on their perception about how their opinion would be received. They are naturally tuned-in to the overall group dynamics as well as the feelings of the individuals that comprise the group.

Relaters are uncomfortable with intangibles. They dislike deviating from the established, proven order... such as when dealing with abstractions. They prefer instead to follow a predetermined, straightforward procedure. They are on firm ground when working with concrete realities such as known products, people, systems and procedures.

They like routine, predictability and defined limits. They tend to anchor the other types with their patience, cooperation and followthrough. They need a firm grip on the facts before feeling ready to proceed, so they prefer systematic information whenever possible. They enjoy team efforts and willingly work to bolster comfortable, efficient working conditions. Relaters support and encourage other members of their group.

At parties, Relaters like to seek out people they know well and are more likely to attend an event with another invitee with whom they are already comfortable. Often, they wind up talking with that same person all night unless they are encouraged to move about more and mingle. They prefer to be approached by others, and often project such a serene, accepting attitude that other people often seek them out.

Relaters dislike being in the spotlight and prefer working behind the scenes and letting others be the stars. They share credit willingly and freely. They choose friends by using the test-of-time method, and Relaters tend to have long-lasting relationships. They often keep in touch with childhood friends, former teachers or even retired doctors. Because familiarity feels so comfortable to them, they may prefer to live in the same neighborhood or area as they did during childhood. Memorabilia tends to mean more to the Relater than it might for some of the other types. Nostalgia makes them feel more connected to the present, giving them a sense that things can stay the same even as time passes by. Consequently, they tend to be possessive about things they own which have personal significance for them and their relationships.

Relaters often use conformity as a means to satisfy their need to feel included by others. They find it easy to listen and have a natural preference for participative communication. One problem facing Relaters is that their aversion to hurting people's feelings may make them respond in an indirect, subtle manner. They find it hard to say "no" and often allow the more assertive types to take advantage of them. Their willingness to listen makes them virtual shock absorbers or sounding boards for the opinions, ideas, experiences and frustrations of others.

Relaters tend to stick with things that have worked in the past. In most aspects of their lives, new or different things do not appeal to them as much as the good old, tried-and-true. The same activities other types perceive as monotonous often appeal to a Relater's desire for repetition. For them familiarity does not breed contempt... but contentment! They find it difficult to reach beyond their comfort zone and take chances.

Although they might remain quiet about resisting change, they may secretly decide to passively revolt.

Relaters display a rather plain, straightforward, seemingly uncomplicated sense of humor. They look at life from a mainstream, commonplace perspective with predictable results in the punch line. Often, the listener can guess the outcome of their joke before it is ever completed.

Persistence is a word often used to describe Relaters. They do not give up easily and can persevere for years. This single-minded resolve can be taken so far as to be seen as stubbornness!

They naturally let little annoyances slide, overlooking things that bother the other types more. Although Relaters exhibit more patience than many of their counterparts, they sometimes allow certain irritations to build up for so long that the burden becomes overwhelming. Because they do not like to rock the boat, they may give in rather than take issue with something. Relaters bruise easily; you may hurt their feelings without realizing it. Relaters can appear almost saintly, simply because they often keep quiet whenever something bothers them. They do not want anyone to dislike them. When the chips are down, they are likely to clam up, going into their own protective shell. They often think that if they say what is on their minds, they may be less likely to keep the friendship. As a result, they will avoid confrontation – their biggest fear – at almost any cost.

Their desire for peace and stability can motivate Relaters to succumb to compromise just to maintain favorable conditions or to avoid conflict. Ironically, instead of jeopardizing their position with others, speaking up and/or taking a stand can sometimes enhance their position... especially with people who may view their tendency to give in as weakness. Voicing their feelings before reaching the end of their tolerance level can actually help Relaters salvage some relationships before it is too late.

Relaters are most comfortable with small groups of people whom they've known for a long time and have had a history of pleasant relationships. They prefer events and activities that are planned (or at least known about) in advance. This provides them with a more predictable experience with defined dimensions… such as when things start and finish, who will be there and what activities may occur.

The best social world for a Relater is one where everyone would act friendly, pleasant and cooperative. No one would strongly disagree, shout, participate in rowdy scenes or talk anyone into anything against his or her will.

Typical social behaviors for the Relater include:

- Building ongoing relationships with a smaller number of people
- Wanting to be involved in (and identified with) their group
- Relating to others on a one-to-one basis, preferably with predictable role behavior by each person
- More casual, low-keyed, amiable relationships
- Giving and then receiving sincere attention
- Seeking stability in their lives through practices such as conformity

Preferred social situations of the Relater include:

- Participating in the group's communication and activities
- Performing regular activities in the same way, at the same time, and at the same place (bowling or golf leagues, bridge club, poker night, etc…)
- Communicating in a conflict-free environment with associates or friends
- Settings that facilitate easy conversations
- Wanting to know how to play games or complete activities through well-defined, step-by-step procedures
- Feeling appreciated and well-liked by others, just for being who they are

THE RELATER STYLE AT WORK

Relaters prefer constancy in their positions and careers, so they can focus on learning to specialize in specific areas and be part of a team. You might find Relaters in the following positions:

- Financial services
- Social worker
- Family doctor/nurse
- Psychologist/counselor
- Residential or community services
- Teacher/professor
- Personal assistant/secretary
- Insurance agent
- Customer service representative

In business and in their personal lives, Relaters take one day at a time and may consciously avoid gambles and uncertainties. They tend to respect the proven status quo and are likely to accommodate others while they trek along. Because stability in the workplace motivates them, Relaters are apt to have the most compatible of all working relationships with each of the four types. Relaters have patience, staying power and persistence, so they commit themselves to making relationships work.

Relaters are extremely uncomfortable with disagreement, often withholding negative observations. They do not want to make waves and they do not want to appear to be know-it-alls. Silently, they may feel as if they're shouldering the lion's share of the duties, but they are unlikely to complain about this to others.

When they need to make a presentation, Relaters prepare thoroughly and organize their material in advance. Since they feel comfortable with proven methods, they like to acquaint themselves thoroughly with each step of a procedure so they can duplicate it later. Sometimes, when this is taken to extreme, this adherence to following instructions and maintaining the status quo can limit their effectiveness.

The Relater's patience and inclination to follow procedures makes them a natural choice for assisting or tutoring others, maintaining existing performance levels, and organizing practices. They often enjoy setting up or implementing guidelines or checklists that enable others to be more organized in their follow-through efforts.

Relaters prefer to resolve problems by working with others as part of a team and using tried-and-true, proven methods. If these tactics fail, the Relater may quietly do nothing. When conflict and stress increase, the Relater's tolerance may decrease, resulting in lowered performance or even absenteeism as a way of coping with the stress.

Relationships, which provide them with security, friendliness, and large doses of routine, attract the Relater. Teaching is a natural career for Relaters as it fills their natural desire for repeated group and one-to-one people contact, preference for sameness and the opportunity to help or support others.

Inherently modest and accommodating, Relaters usually think their actions speak for themselves. Inwardly, they may want to divulge a personal triumph, but they won't volunteer it or brag about it. Rather than asking for a promotion, the Relater will quietly hope the supervisor notices their good work and offers them a reward.

Since Relaters seek security and inclusion within a group, they can contribute to the workplace with their natural organizing talents, consistent pace, and desire to fit in. They favor work relationships on a casual, first name basis, and enjoy developing more in-depth friendships with selected co-workers. They contribute to harmony in the office, but sometimes become overly dependent on using the same old methods repeatedly even when they work less and less effectively.

The Relater is the optimistic realist among the four types. As a pragmatist in this regard, they like to do routine things with familiar people to maintain the same situation. They perform regularly and deliberately toward this end of holding onto continuity, peace and orderliness. Changes and surprises make them uncomfortable because they alter the current formulas. Relaters prefer refinement to dramatic changes.

Typical business characteristics of the Relater include:

- Needs to know the order of procedures; fears the unknown
- Slow and steady; builds strong and deep relationships, but with fewer people

- Operates well as a member of the work group
- Motivated by customary, known, proven practices
- Oriented toward more concrete, repeatable actions
- Wants order and stability in the workplace
- Focuses on how and when to do things
- Works in a steady and predictable manner
- Likes a long-term relationship with their place of business and their fellow employees

Preferred business situations of the Relater include:

- Performing the same kinds of duties day after day (no matter the importance of the type of work involved)
- Working cooperatively with others to achieve common results
- Safe, risk-free environments
- Stable, steady, low-key environment which has a minimum of changes
- Knowing each step toward completing their duties within a defined framework of time and resources
- Making decisions by group consensus or other accepted practices rather than only by themselves
- Feeling like an appreciated, contributing member of the work group

THE RELATER SALESPERSON

The natural style of the Relater salesperson is to build relationships and to progress slowly and steadily through the sales process. They are very concerned with maintaining the relationship and making sure that they have the best possible solution for their customer. They spend a lot of time getting to know the customer personally and seek to understand their personal preferences and dislikes. They also use their listening talents to get an in-depth picture of the customer's needs and wants.

The Relater's ideal sales position is one that requires strong customer relationships and a service orientation. Systems or services that require months (or years) of repeated, incremental work to respond to known needs (and involve the same decision makers) are perfect for the Relater. Relaters maintain relationships with high levels of service, personal involvement, and attention to details.

The Relater salesperson seldom pushes for a close ... or seldom needs to. Through their painstaking needs identification process and emphasis on knowing and understanding their customers, getting the customer's commitment flows out as an almost evolutionary part of the sales process.

Relaters are most successful dealing with systems or products that allow them to interact with relatively few prospects and spend a longer period making sure the product solution fits for each prospect. They tend to provide their customers with lots of data as well as input about the purchase decision. They enjoy sales or service work that requires a team approach.

There is one weakness of the Relater as a salesperson: while it is true that their greatest strength is reading others, it can get in the way when working toward confirming a sale. They become worried about applying too much pressure or what may happen to the customer after the sale. They ask themselves, "What happens if the customer does not like the house, car, jewelry, etc… that they bought from me? I would feel just terrible if they were not completely happy." This issue is one that a Relater salesperson must learn to deal with to become more successful.

THE RELATER CUSTOMER

The Relater customer needs to have a relationship based upon personal assurances and trust prior to making a buying decision. Relaters tend to assemble a buying committee of advisors to help them make the decision because they want everyone affected by the purchase to have a say in the decision. Relaters are seldom in a hurry to make decisions and will become turned off by pushy, aggressive behavior.

Relaters respond to friendly attention and efforts to make them feel like a part of the customer/vendor team. They need to be personally at ease with the salesperson. They also want to understand how the operations of the company behind the salesperson might affect them. They want the salesperson to listen and be sensitive to their needs and situational requirements. Once they have established a strong relationship, they are likely to remain loyal to the salesperson… even in the face of competition.

Relaters expect salespeople to be available to make presentations to other people within the organization who might have an interest in the purchasing decision. They want to make sure that the decision will be completely accepted by their organization before making a final commitment. They also want assurance that they can depend on the salesperson to honor all commitments.

Relaters have difficulty saying "no" and may make excuses or create delays in order to get out of a difficult sales situation. They expect the salesperson to be in tune with their needs and feelings. When they feel that the salesperson does not understand or sincerely care about their situation, they withdraw or change the subject. There is one exception to this tendency: Relaters will say "no" rather quickly when they get the sense that a salesperson is lying or trying to sell them something that may be harmful to their company, family or personal security.

Relaters at a Glance:
- Concerned with stability
- Thinks things through in an orderly manner
- Wants documentation and facts
- Needs personal involvement
- Takes action and make decisions slowly
- Needs to know the step-by-step sequence
- Avoids risks and changes
- Dislikes interpersonal conflict
- Works slowly, but cohesively with others
- Tries to accommodate others
- Wants tranquility and peace
- Seeks security and sense of belonging

- Enjoys teamwork
- Wants to know they are appreciated
- Possesses excellent counseling talents

Is there someone you know who is a Relater? What did you read to help you identify that person as a Relater and not a Director, Socializer, or Thinker? Is this person also in a position or career that is typical of Relaters? What did the book suggest it would take to convert the Relater customer into a loyal customer?

BEHAVIORAL STYLES QUIZ

Now that you have read Section I that described the characteristics of the four behavioral styles, it is time to test your memory and apply what you learned. Below are a series of statements. Read each one and decide which behavioral style would make such a statement. Hint; there are two statements for each of the four behavioral styles. To see if you correctly identified the statements from the four behavioral styles, please visit: **www.platinumrule.com/ section1quiz.html**

1. I do not need any help; I have it all under control. _____
2. You may quit work today at 5 pm and not one minute before or after that time. _____
3. I would have done better in school if I had not talked so much during class. _____
4. Here is what you should do to solve your problem because it is what I would do to solve it. _____
5. How will the managers' families be affected if we routinely require them to work more than 60 hours per week? _____
6. I know, let's all come to work on Friday wearing funny hats to celebrate the end of the work week! _____
7. Please stop arguing and learn to get along with each other for goodness sake. _____
8. The most logical way to increase profits at our restaurant is to buy the cheapest goods possible. _____

SECTION II

identifying the four behavioral styles of customers

In this section, you will learn two simple techniques that will get you well on your way to reading the behavioral styles of others. You will discover ways to determine whether each individual is more Direct or Indirect and more Open or Guarded. In doing so, you can quickly determine if each and every customer is a Director, Relater, Socializer or Thinker.

Preface to this section: One of the people who reviewed the manuscript for this book said that we were pointing out more negatives about "Indirect" behaviors than we did for "Direct" behaviors. He may be right (of course, he happens to be Indirect). However, the point of this book is to teach the reader how to build rapport, establish credibility and how to make more sales. If you find that your style is "Indirect," please be aware that your roundabout, slow-paced delivery style may frustrate Direct (faster pace) people during conversations. Direct people may become bored or distracted during conversations that are monotonous, slow and/or lack focus. Conversely, Indirect people often view Direct people (fast taking and/or animated) with skepticism. Read on with an open mind and a desire to learn how to communicate your ideas effectively with everyone you encounter.

Note: *The Platinum Rule* is based upon observable behaviors, NOT "personalities" or "temperaments." This distinction is critical because human beings may often change their behavior in the middle of a conversation. When you learn to adapt to the behavior that you are witnessing, you will stay in rapport with that person. People's personalities are deeply ingrained and slow to change, but behaviors can change in the blink of an eye. The way a person is acting at each moment in time will dictate how you should be selling to them.

5

identifying your customers' styles

There are two "dimensions" that help us determine another person's style:

1. How "Direct" or "Indirect" their behaviors are, and;
2. How "Open" or "Guarded" they are in revealing private thoughts.

When you correctly read both of these dimensions, you have determined the other person's natural style and are well on their way to a better relationship.

DIRECT BEHAVIORS

The dimension of "directness" deals with the amount of involvement a person uses to meet his needs by seeking to influence people and situations. Directness means the tendency to move forward, outwardly expressing thoughts, feelings or expectations.

Direct people come on strong, take the social initiative and create a powerful first impression. They tend to be assertive, fast-paced people who make swift decisions and take risks. They can easily become impatient with others who do not keep up with their pace. As active people who talk a lot, they appear confident and sometimes dominant. Direct people

61

tend to express opinions readily and make emphatic statements. Such individuals try to shape their environment and relationships directly. "Tell Stevenson that I want to talk to him ASAP!" barks a Direct person; a more Indirect may ask his secretary to see if Mr. Stevenson would please come to his office, when it is convenient.

Direct people are faster paced, more assertive and more competitive than Indirect people. At worst, these tendencies sometimes transform into hastiness, combativeness, or a lower awareness of others' needs. More outspoken, talkative, and dominant, Direct people are extroverts who focus their attention on interests within their immediate environment. In other words... action! They tend to work and play faster. When at a social gathering, they're the ones who introduce themselves as a natural way of seeking to influence others.

Direct people prefer to make rapid decisions, often becoming impatient when things do not move fast enough or do not go their way. Checking for errors is something other people can do; it's too time-consuming and self-involving for Direct people. Instead of checking, they busily rush into new areas where the more Indirect may fear to tread. In fact, they often rush into so many new areas that their time seems to evaporate into thin air. That's one reason why they have difficulty consistently being prompt... because something comes up at the office or somewhere else. Meanwhile, their more punctual, Indirect friends learn to busy themselves with time killers, such as projects or magazines, while waiting for their more easily side-tracked companions.

Direct people may enjoy taking risks and want results now (or yesterday). Risks are a way of life with them. Not only are they less worried about rocking the boat, they'll often tip it over and splash around in the hot water they helped create. They crave excitement, so they do as much as possible to get it.

The more Direct type feels that if they throw enough stuff against the wall, something has to stick. "Who cares if the output isn't perfect? Did it work?" they ask. If so, that is the direction they were looking for. Quantity beats quality (within limits known only to them) most days of the week. Therefore, they are likely to tolerate a higher error rate than their Indirect counterparts to gain a higher number of trial opportunities, even if their success ratio is lower. They generally figure that the number of successes is more important than the percentage of successes. They play for high stakes results with sizzle.

Direct people are the "home run" crushers, not "get on base," high-average hitters. Direct people "swing for the fences" with gusto! They focus on the one-in-ten grand slam while quickly erasing the memories of the strikeouts that occur between connecting with the "big one."

Anyone involved in telemarketing or outside sales realizes that the road to success is littered with rejection and setbacks. Direct people excel in these jobs because they're able to take "no's"… they simply go out and find more prospects. Aware that the "yes's" are out there somewhere, they're determined to unearth them. The Direct salesperson says to himself, "The odds are definitely in my favor now. I'm due to land one!" Indirect people tend to take "no's" as personal rejections, responding by examining other alternatives which do not force them to stick their own necks out again. The Indirect salesperson says, "Maybe if I send out a direct mail letter first, then follow up by phone, I'll increase my chances of getting a yes." An Indirect salesperson sometimes invests too much time and effort in low-payoff marketing activities (sending letters, brochures, etc…) because it is "selling indirectly" without having to hear "No" from the prospect.

Direct people point, finger jab, or otherwise more observably express themselves. They are verbally intense and expressive. "Take it or leave it," a Direct person exclaims, "this is the way it's going to be, so get used to it!" They emphasize their points of view with confident-sounding vocal intonations and assertive body language.

Speaking with conviction, fast-talking, Direct people like to tell – not ask – about situations. If you want to know the answer, just ask them. They can even become brutally blunt: "Are you sure that's a custom suit? It looks more like a horse blanket … ha, ha, ha. I'm just kidding, of course!" While other Direct types might join in the laughter, the Indirect person is sensitive to feelings and is likely to be thinking, "Gosh, I wonder what would possess someone to come right out and say something like that?"

Impatient and quick-paced, Direct people jump into things, so they get into more "iffy" situations than their Indirect counterparts do. Just as the songs of the sirens lured sailors to their doom, the windows of opportunity beckon to Direct people. Sometimes they net huge results and sometimes they encounter dramatic disasters. Wherever inclination takes them, their natural tendency is to do their own thing... as long as it includes doing something.

When windows of opportunity do crack open, the Direct types cannot wait to tell somebody about their idea or plan of action. Therefore, they seek out willing listeners – usually of the Indirect variety – about the opportunity... even if it includes a gray area in policies and procedures. The Indirect types listen and often reply with a cautious, "It sounds interesting, but it also raises a lot of questions. Have you asked anyone else for their opinion... like the boss?"

The Direct replies, "Ask the boss? Forget that... he might say "no!" Then what would I do? My hands would be tied." The truly Direct person's motto might be, "It's easier to ask forgiveness afterwards than seek permission beforehand."

Summary: Remember... one "dimension" is not "better" than the other. People who are more direct in their behavior have certain advantages than those who are less direct. However, they also have disadvantages, especially when dealing with people who are less direct than they are. We are not "picking on" people of certain behaviors, we are simply pointing out behaviors.

INDIRECT BEHAVIORS

On the opposite side of the Directness spectrum, we find the quieter and reserved group... the Indirect people. They may be seen as more easygoing, or at least more self-contained in keeping their views to themselves. Indirect people ask questions and listen more than they talk.

They typically do not share their opinions or concerns. When asked to take a stand, they may either make tentative statements or say nothing at all. They often appear more objective, introverted and indecisive.

When taken to an extreme, these positive traits can be viewed as negative ones: indecisive, tight-lipped, unassertive behaviors. Indirect people act in less confronting, less demanding, less assertive, and less socially competitive manner than their Direct counterparts. They allow others to take the social initiative. For instance, when they want to go to the movies or a restaurant, they might think to themselves, "I'd rather see that new romantic-comedy movie." However, when their spouse or date suggests the latest action-adventure epic, they often go along without mentioning their own interests. If they really, truly disagreed with the suggestion, they may go so far as to say, "Gee, I heard that other movie was really well received. Are you sure you wouldn't rather try that one tonight?" Usually, their desires remain unspoken.

Indirect people tend to be more sensitive toward risk: moving cautiously, meditating on their decisions and avoiding big changes. As a result, they often avoid taking bold chances or acting spontaneously. After all, what is the best way to keep from failing? One way is to do nothing until you are convinced it will be an improvement. In other words, only do sure things. Sure things result in a higher success ratio, so they are choices that are more attractive for Indirect people.

When Indirect people flop, they tend to take the setback personally. They are likely to internalize or privately reassess any failure, often wondering if there's something wrong with them. "How could I have been so stupid?" the Indirect asks himself after a setback. Just give them a hint that something is going wrong, and reserved folks may engage in negative self-talk for days. By contrast, the Direct type seldom has extra time to spend looking back and reflecting on such considerations.

Indirect people tend to move at a slower, more measured pace than Direct people do. For them, "sooner or later" is good enough. They speak and respond more slowly since they are more cautious or stability-focused when considering change. They tend to seek increases in security while looking for ways to reduce fear. If their behavior becomes too measured, detractors (usually Direct people) may view this as dragging their feet, or even lacking interest.

Predictability is more important to such Indirect people, so they tend to weigh pros and cons, attend to details and fact-find. Caught in a gray area with no clear-cut guidelines, they usually ask for clarification or permission before they take action. They seek to meet their needs by accommodating the requirements of their environment. They tend to operate according to established formats and rules, so when you make an appointment with an Indirect person, you can expect him to show up on time, or possibly be waiting on you!

Indirect people tend to communicate by asking or observing instead of stating or showing. Their questions attempt to clarify, support, or seek more information. They prefer qualified statements and speak more tentatively, often taking a roundabout or systematic approach. "According to some sources," or "It seems to like/as though," and "Perhaps another way of looking at this situation might be to consider...," are common ways Indirects preface a comment, idea or opinion. If they do not like something, they respond subtly: "Well, other people have often commented about how good you look in your navy pinstripe suit," is an Indirect's way of telling you she dislikes the brown suit you are wearing. They reserve the right to express their opinions or keep them to themselves. In some cases, they can also act like impregnable vaults when they do not feel like sharing information.

Based on what you've just read, what words or images now come to mind when thinking about "direct" versus "indirect" behaviors? Knowing the differences between these two types of behaviors will get you one step closer to becoming a more successful salesperson. Give this some thought before reading further.

TYPICAL BEHAVIORS

Direct people, to borrow a Wall Street metaphor, are the "bulls." They can be forcefully expressive, Type-A personalities who confront conflict, change, risk and decision-making head on... without giving it a second thought.

Direct people are outspoken communicators and often dominate business meetings. They will tell you their opinions even if you do not want to hear them, and if they want your opinion, they'll give it to you!

Direct people are competitive, impatient, and at times, confrontational. They bulldoze or zoom their way through life. They often argue for the sake of arguing. They hold eye contact longer than average and possess an air of confidence. Their handshakes are memorable for their firmness.

Direct people thrive on accomplishment and are not overly concerned with rules and policies. They are more likely to look for expedient ways to attain their goals than to focus on obstacles or setbacks. Ambiguity does not deter them; it encourages them. They take advantage of gray areas and call them "windows of opportunity."

Indirect people are Wall Street "bears." They approach risk, decision-making, and change cautiously. They are the "meek who inherit the earth." They are the Type-B personalities who are slow-paced and low-key in their approach with others.

Indirect people are tentative, reserved communicators. They are not eager, high-profile contributors in meetings (although their insights can be very valuable). When solicited for their opinions, they often preface their statements with qualifications such as: "Have we all considered what might happen if..." or "According to the theories/principles of..."

Indirect people avoid open conflict whenever possible. They are more diplomatic, patient and cooperative. On unimportant issues, they will conform rather than argue. When they have strong convictions about an issue, however, they will stand their ground... often simply by withholding the approval being sought from them. They often base their delays on the need for additional research, pending contracts, or missing data. When they are less than completely convinced, they subconsciously weigh an issue's importance against the discomfort of confrontation.

Indirect people are low profile, reserved and gentle. For example, their handshakes are sometimes soft, and they speak at a slower pace and lower volume than direct people. They do not take the initiative at social gatherings, but prefer to wait for others to approach them.

READING BEHAVIORAL STYLES

For those who did not take the online Platinum Rule Assessment at http://www.PlatinumRuleGroup.com , this next section is a quick way to identify your style (and the styles of others). In doing so, you are well on your way to having better relationships with people at work, socially and at home.

As you seek to know your style – and that of others – bear in mind that people are not simple creatures; they can be infinitely complex. Every person possesses each of the styles to some degree; so expect to find shades of gray... not black and white. However, people do have one dominant style that rises above the other three that gives them their uniqueness. Yes, there are instances where a person may be direct in one setting (work) but indirect when at home; they may be open with their significant other, but guarded with co-workers. So, always deal with the person in the behavior that they are demonstrating at the particular moment in time you are interacting with them.

Before you learn how to "read" the behavioral styles of others, identify your own style. On the following page, you will find a chart of Indirect and Direct behaviors. Read each description of behaviors and check the one that most closely describes your behavior. For example, do you tend to "avoid risks" or "take risks?" Check the one that most describes your behavior. Remember, one is not "better" than the other; this is simply a way to begin developing the skill of reading the behavioral style of yourself and others.

(Check the box if this behavior sounds most like you)

"Indirect Behaviors"	or	"Direct Behaviors"	
I tend to be slower paced	or	I tend to be faster paced.	
I tend to listen more than talk.	or	I tend to talk more than listen.	
I am reluctant to directly express my opinions.	or	I find it easy to directly express my opinions.	
I usually react slowly when faced with new situations or decisions.	or	I usually react quickly when faced with new situations or decisions.	
I make decisions after all the facts are available.	or	I make decisions whether or not all the facts are available.	
I come across as less assertive than others.	or	I come across as more assertive than others.	
I tend to "bite my tongue" when I don't agree with someone.	or	I tend to "speak my mind" when I don't agree with someone.	
I get frustrated when things move too quickly.	or	I get impatient when things move too slowly.	
I generally avoid conflict.	or	I do not avoid conflict.	
TOTAL "INDIRECT" CHECKMARKS		TOTAL "DIRECT" CHECKMARKS	

First, having checked the items that most describe you, are you more Indirect or more Direct?

Next, determining whether you express yourself in a more "open" or "guarded" manner will enable you to pinpoint your behavioral style (and that of other people).

Open or Guarded?

DO THEY WEAR THEIR HEART ON THEIR SLEEVE...
OR HIDE A CARD UP THEIR SLEEVE?

While Direct individuals attempt to control the people around them, Indirect types prefer to exercise control on their environment. In addition to Direct/Indirect, the other dimension of observable behavior that people tend to exhibit is Open or Guarded. This second behavioral scale explains the internal motivating goals behind our daily actions. The Open/Guarded dimension relates to why we do the things we do in the way we do them.

When combined, these two scales explain both the tendency to reveal our thoughts and feelings, plus the degree to which we tend to support other people's expressions of their thoughts and feelings.

Open Behaviors

Open people are motivated by their relationships and feelings. They are open to getting to know people and they tend to make decisions based on feelings, experiences and relationships.

The Open person is emotionally available and shows it by talking with his body, using more vocal inflections, making continual eye contact, and communicating in terms of feelings more than the Guarded types. Other Open clues are animated facial expressions, a large amount of hand and body movement, a flexible time perspective and immediate, non-verbal feedback. Open people also like to tell, or listen to, stories and anecdotes and make personal contact. They are comfortable with emotions and openly express their joy, sadness, confusion and other emotions.

Open people respond to passing interests – their own and others' – even though this may take them away from the business or subject at hand. They like to make conversations enjoyable, so they often stray from the subject to discuss personal experiences and interests. As long as it's in the ballpark, they figure it's probably relevant. An Open person might say, "That reminds me of the time uncle Jed got stuck on the Garden State Freeway in a snowstorm . . ." Exaggeration of details just adds interest by fully depicting personal experiences.

Open types are also more accepting about time usage. Their time perspective is organized around the needs of people first and tasks second, so they are more flexible about how others use their time than the Guarded types. "I'm sorry I'm late," explains an Open person, "but Jimmy was crying this morning because Jason broke his science project. I had to write a note to his teacher and cheer him up before I dropped him off at school."

Guarded Behaviors

If Open types seem like an open book, Guarded people tend to be more poker-faced. Guarded types like to play their cards close to the vest in order to increase their probability of getting the upper hand and decreasing the probability of appearing foolish. Guarded types are motivated by completing tasks and accomplishing their goals. They usually like to keep their distance, both physically and emotionally. They will not readily touch you and they do not like being touched by strangers, casual friends or business associates. People often comment that once they get to know a Guarded person, "He's a really great guy; it's just hard breaking through his thick shell."

Guarded people tend to stand further away from you (even when shaking hands) than Open types. They have a strong sense of personal space and they dislike it when someone invades their territory. They feel invaded when you take something from their desk, use personal items without permission, or call meetings (requiring their time) without asking their input.

Guarded people show less facial expression, displaying limited or controlled hand and body movement, and adhere to a more time-disciplined agenda. They push for facts and details, they focus on the issues and tasks; they keep their personal feelings private. They are not naturally "touchy-feely," and they tend to respond stiffly if anyone touches them. Unlike their Open counterparts, they give less wide-ranging, non-verbal feedback.

In contrast to Open people, Guarded types typically place higher priority on getting things done. They prefer working with things rather than working with people. Typical comments from a Guarded person include, "I can't talk now, Frank," or "I have a two o'clock deadline to meet," or "I'll let you know when I have time to do that." or "I'll get back to you later after I've had more time to think about it."

The more Guarded types like structure; they like to know what to expect. Additionally, they prefer to have control over results within a structured environment. When negatively motivated, they can be viewed as coercive, restrictive or overbearing. They prefer to stick with an agenda… at least if it's their own.

Because time equals money to Guarded individuals, they are more disciplined about how other people use their time. In part, this explains their tendency not to show, discuss, or willingly listen to thoughts and feelings to the extent Open people do. Guarded types are more matter-of-fact, with more fixed expectations of people and situations. Just as facts place second for Open people, feelings take the back seat for the more Guarded types. You might say that Open people tend to experience life by tuning in to the concerns or feeling states (of themselves and others) and then reacting to them. By contrast, Guarded people focus on the tasks or ideas in question and respond primarily to those stimuli.

Guarded people prefer to know where a conversation is heading. Idle, non-directed chitchat is uncomfortable for them. If Open types stray from the subject, Guarded people find a way to bring them back on track. They usually need clarity before they move on to the next topic. If you get off the subject, they are likely to ask, "Can you sum that up for me?" or "What is the key point you're trying to make?"

Because of their different priorities, Guarded types often perceive Open people as time-wasters or indecisive. Conversely, Open types may view Guarded people as cold, unsympathetic, or self-involved. As a result, misunderstandings can quickly grow out of proportion when we do not discern and respond to the source of the differences… the inner motivating needs that drive our personal styles of behavior.

You have just read about "open" and "guarded" behaviors. What words or images now come to mind when thinking about open versus guarded behaviors? Are you able to fill in the blanks of the following sentence with two or three descriptors for each one? "I would describe people exhibiting open behaviors as those who are _____, _____, and/or _____. People exhibiting guarded behaviors as being _____, _____, and/or _____."

TYPICAL BEHAVIORS

Open people often become physically and emotionally closer to people. During a conversation, they may almost stand on your toes. They are huggers, hand shakers, "touchers" and natural, easy smilers (never a forced grin). They are outgoing and develop deeper relationships with others.

Open folks are informal and enjoy quickly breaking down the walls of formality. They like to swap first names as soon as possible, and they prefer relaxed, warm relationships.

Open people enjoy free-flowing, enjoyable conversations. They can often be as interested in your brother-in-law's surgery as they are in discussing the business on the formal agenda. Interaction within a conversation is more important than content to them.

Additionally, Open people dislike strict structuring of their time, and they rarely mind when other people take up a lot of their time. In fact, they often balk at imposed schedules and agendas and prefer to "go with the flow."

Open types are feeling-oriented decision makers. They are in touch with their intuitions as well as the feelings of others. They come to their decisions through their interaction with others rather than only by their own cogitations.

In contrast, Guarded people do not readily show their emotions. They are more physically rigid and less expressive than their Open counterparts are. They like to present an image of being in control of themselves and not flustered by other people or situations. If you were a stand-up comedian, you wouldn't want an audience full of Guarded people. Like most of their emotions, their laughter is kept primarily on the inside.

Guarded people keep their distance, physically and psychologically. They are harder to get to know than Open types. They tend to remain aloof and value their privacy, especially in the beginning stages of a relationship. They arrange their offices to provide formal efficiency and a comfortable distance from visitors. With strangers, they prefer to keep everything on a professional, business level.

Guarded people are task-oriented. A conversation with a Guarded person will rarely stray from the topic that initiated the contact. They dislike interruptions from their agendas, unless they initiate the diversion.

Guarded people are fact-oriented decision makers. They respond to proof and hard evidence. In the workplace, they prefer to work alone and put less emphasis on opinions and feelings of others. On the surface, they appear to operate in an intellectual mode rather than an emotional mode.

Guarded people are champions of time and priorities management. They are the efficiency experts of the world, who create and follow rigid plans and schedules. They implore other people to respect their time and not to waste it.

Below is a list of Open and Guarded behaviors. Read each set of behavior descriptions on the list and check the one that most closely describes you. For example, are you more "relaxed, warm and animated" or more "formal and proper?" Check the one that describes you then do the same for each pair of descriptors. As with the previous checklist, remember that one is not "better" than the other is; it is simply a way of beginning to develop the skill of reading the behavioral style of yourself and others.

(Check the box if this behavior sounds most like you)

"Open Behaviors"	or	"Guarded Behaviors"	
I find it easy to share and discuss personal feelings with others.	or	I prefer to keep personal feelings private, sharing them only when necessary.	
I prefer to socialize with others before getting tasks started.	or	I prefer getting tasks completed before socializing with others.	
I tend to exhibit animated facial expressions during conversations with others.	or	I tend NOT to exhibit animated facial expressions during conversations with others.	
I tend to get motivated when dealing with people on a daily basis.	or	I tend to get stressed when dealing with people on a daily basis.	
I prefer to work with other people or in groups.	or	I prefer to work independently.	
I am easy to approach in new social situations.	or	I am more standoffish in new social situations.	
I am easy to get to know.	or	It takes time to get to know me.	
I value feelings over facts.	or	I value facts over feelings.	
I usually am NOT time disciplined.	or	I am mostly time disciplined.	
TOTAL "OPEN" CHECKMARKS		TOTAL "GUARDED" CHECKMARKS	

Now that you have completed both checklists, you can determine your behavioral style:

- If you rated yourself as "Open" and "Direct," you are a Socializer.

- If you rated yourself as "Guarded" and "Direct," you are a Director.
- If you rated yourself as "Indirect" and "Open," you are a Relater.
- If you rated yourself as "Indirect" and "Guarded," you are a Thinker.

Another way to verify the rating you gave yourself is by taking the online assessment at www.PlatinumRuleGroup.com/assessment. This assessment is free and provides verification of your self-assessment. If they match, you may be well on your way to identifying your behavioral style, the first step to becoming a more successful salesperson.

READING THE STYLES OF CUSTOMERS (OR ANY OTHER PERSON)

We can best demonstrate the process of reading the style of a customer through a scenario of a salesperson preparing for a sales call. Remember, each new encounter, whether in person or over the phone, should begin with you seeking answers to the two basic questions that will help you get a sense of the other person's behavioral style. These answers shape how you should adapt to the style of that individual from that point forward to increase rapport and improve your probability of making a sale. The two key questions you should try to answer as quickly as possible are:

1. Is this person more Direct or more Indirect?
2. Is this person more Open or more Guarded?

For instance, let's say you are getting ready to call on Sarah Jones, the general manager of Beta Corporation; a prospect for a new telephone system. You reflect back on your preliminary contacts with Ms. Jones (or conversations with those who know her) to see if you think she was Direct or Indirect. You review the continuum of clues to get a better picture of her preferences.

When you originally called Ms. Jones, her voice sounded impatient and rushed, and she talked rapidly. She quickly told you that she was satisfied with her present phone system, that it was budget season and she really didn't have time to meet with you. You requested just a couple of minutes to ask a few questions about her business and she impatiently agreed. During this exploration, you discovered that Beta Corporation is experiencing very rapid growth and Ms. Jones admits that she is not sure about the expansion capabilities of her present phone system. You offer to get the information for her and present it along with a description of your new, unlimited-expansion phone system. She agrees to meet with you for 15 minutes the following Wednesday at 11:15 a.m.

As you think through this meeting, you realize that Ms. Jones exhibited several "Direct" traits: she talked fast, quickly expressed her opinions, displayed impatience and quickly made a decision to listen to a brief presentation. Her continuum checklist may look similar to the one on the following page.

(Check each behavior you noticed)

"Indirect Behaviors"	or	"Direct Behaviors"	
She appeared to be slower paced.	or	She appeared to be faster paced.	X
She listened more than she talked.	or	She talked more than she listened.	
She often made qualified statements: "According to my sources…" or, "I think in some cases…"	or	She often made emphatic statements: "This is so!" or, "I'm quite positive that…"	
She appeared to be patient and/or cooperative.	or	She appeared to be impatient and/or competitive.	X
She offered a weak handshake and looked away often during your conversation.	or	She offered a strong handshake and confidently maintained eye contact throughout the conversation.	X
Her questions tended to be for clarification, support and/or to gain more information.	or	Her questions seemed to be rhetorical… to emphasize points or to challenge information.	
She used very subdued hand gestures and spoke in a rather quiet, monotone voice.	or	She frequently used hand gestures and voice intonations while making points.	X
0 TOTAL "INDIRECT" CHECKMARKS		TOTAL "DIRECT" CHECKMARKS	4

You refer to the Platinum Grid (below) and reflect upon your observations.

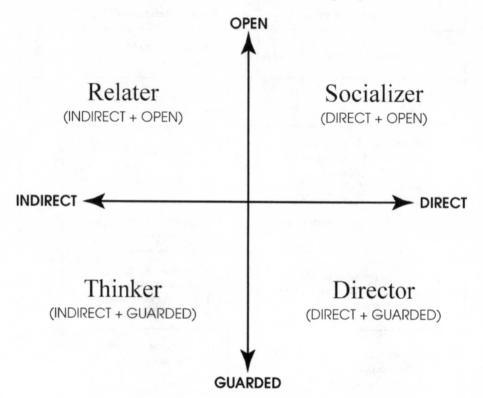

Although a few items on the checklist could not be determined from your first meeting, you determine that your best bet in responding to her is as a Direct person. You would want to follow-up with further exploration on items such as Ms. Jones' approach to "risk" as part of the sales process. However, you have made the decision that Ms. Jones is Direct, and you have eliminated the two styles that fall on the left side of the Platinum Grid.

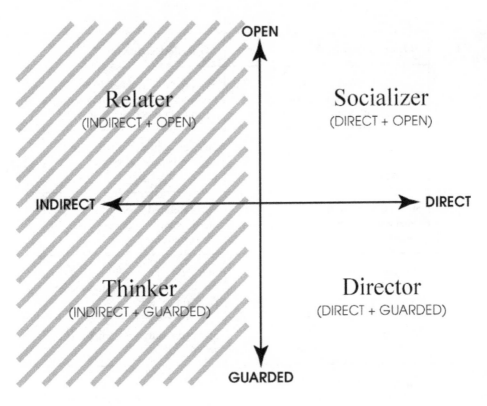

If Ms. Jones is Direct, then she must be either a Socializer or a Director. Again, you think through your conversation and review the description of the Open/Guarded continuum.

You realize that Ms. Jones was very task-oriented and spent little time on personal matters or chitchat. She seemed very formal, never suggesting you use her first name and was very concerned about the total time requirements of your appointment. Your Open/Guarded continuum checklist may look similar to this one:

(Check each behavior you noticed)

	"Open Behaviors"	or	"Guarded Behaviors"	
	It seemed easy for her to share and discuss her personal feelings with you.	or	She preferred to keep her personal feelings private, sharing them only when necessary.	X
	She seemed comfortable socializing with you before getting down to business.	or	She got right down to business and made little effort to socialize.	X
	She exhibited animated facial expressions during the conversation.	or	She exhibited very little facial expression during the conversations.	X
	Her conversation often strayed from the subject at hand.	or	She focused the conversation on the relevant issues and stayed right on subject.	X
	She came across as warm and relaxed.	or	She came across as cool, formal and proper	
	She walked out to greet you; offering a warm handshake at a close distance.	or	Her greeting was "officious" (a quick handshake offered from a distance).	
	She didn't seem to notice the passing of time.	or	She seemed to keep a sharp eye on the time.	X
0	TOTAL "OPEN" CHECKMARKS		TOTAL "GUARDED" CHECKMARKS	5

You decide that Ms. Jones is a Guarded type. As a result, when you combine her Direct style with her Guarded behavior pattern, this leads you to conclude that she is more likely to be a Director.

Let's try a different example: You call Sam Greenwood, the vice president of training of a large financial institution, to set up an appointment to discuss training software. Mr. Greenwood answers his own phone in a notably quiet voice. He talks in a soft, moderately paced voice and listens patiently as you explain who recommended that you call. After your introduction, he spends a minute or two talking about his friendship with the person who referred you. He asks you several questions about you (personally) and about your company. He addresses you by your first name. When you ask for an appointment, he says his schedule is flexible and he asks what time would be convenient for you.

Again using the process of elimination, you look at the descriptors of Direct/Indirect and decide that Mr. Greenwood's soft voice, patience and the amount of time he spent listening places him on the Indirect side of the dimension. That eliminates the behavioral styles on the right side of the quadrant: Socializer and Director. When you look at the Open/Guarded descriptions, you remember that Mr. Greenwood spent time talking about his friendship with the person who referred you, he seemed interested in getting to know more about you, he had a warm, friendly style, and he was flexible about setting up a meeting time convenient for you. You decide that he must be more Open than Guarded… which would make him a Relater.

TYPICAL BEHAVIORS

To help you understand and remember these two dimensions, here is a brief quiz for each dimension. Try not to look at the answers below until you have answered the following questions. For each item, mark an X under the Direct or Indirect heading.

Direct or Indirect?

	Indirect		Direct
1. Talks Fast	_____	or	_____
2. Listens Carefully	_____	or	_____
3. Firm Handshake	_____	or	_____
4. Speaks Softly	_____	or	_____
5. Uses Emphatic Gestures	_____	or	_____
6. Asks Clarification Questions	_____	or	_____
7. Longer Eye Contact	_____	or	_____
8. Makes Tentative Statements	_____	or	_____
9. Expresses Views Readily	_____	or	_____
10. Waits to be Introduced	_____	or	_____

(Answers to "Direct or Indirect?": Odd numbers – Direct; Even numbers – Indirect)

Open or Guarded?

	Open		Guarded
1. Animated Facial Expressions	_____	or	_____
2. Expects Other to Arrive on Time	_____	or	_____
3. Tells Stories and Anecdotes	_____	or	_____
4. Conversations Focused on Tasks	_____	or	_____
5. Shares Personal Feelings Easily	_____	or	_____
6. More Formal, Proper Style and Dress ...	_____	or	_____
7. Asks How You Feel About Things	_____	or	_____
8. Poker-Faced, Does Not Smile Easily	_____	or	_____
9. Comfortable with Touching	_____	or	_____
10. Want to See Evidence	_____	or	_____

(Answers to "Open or Guarded?": Odd numbers - Open; Even numbers - Guarded)

Once you have made a preliminary assessment of the customer's behavioral style (by asking the two key questions of "Direct" or "Indirect" and "Open" or "Guarded"), you should factor in other behaviors and environmental clues to help you confirm your assessment of their behavior.

ENVIRONMENTAL CLUES TO STYLE

Once you have determined your customer's style (by observing his behaviors and manner of communication), you can look for environmental clues that may even further confirm your conclusion.

Look at your customer's office. How is it decorated and arranged? What items are on the desk? Is it messy, organized into neat piles or spotlessly clean? What types of things are on the walls and in their bookshelf? What seating arrangement does this customer seem to prefer and find most comfortable?

Environmental clues offer important information, but should not be used as the sole basis for determining one's style. In many situations, environment may be determined more by the culture of the organization than by your client. Looking for environmental clues is a way to enhance and corroborate the identification made by observing behavior. This observation also helps you glean clues about an organization's culture and style.

Director Environments

A Director's desk is likely to be busy with paperwork, projects and material separated into organized piles. Both their in-baskets and out-baskets typically bulge with busywork. They also tend to surround themselves with trophies, awards, and other evidence of personal achievement. Everything about this office signals hustle, bustle, formality and power.

The Director's preferred power decoration generally includes a large chair behind a massive desk; providing separation from visitors. Walls often display plaques, degrees, awards and other evidence of success as well as large event calendars or project tracking charts. Any photos will probably be of them with dignitaries or celebrities that communicate their level of status or importance. If family photos are displayed, they are usually placed behind the Director, so they do not distract from business at hand. You might even find inspirational sayings such as, "If I do not find the road to success, I will build it myself!"

Directors are more formal and prefer to keep their distance physically and psychologically. They are sensitive about their personal space and do not like to have people get too close. The typical office arrangement is formal with seating that is face-to-face with a big "power desk" separating the Director from his visitors.

Socializer Environments

Socializers respond to visual stimuli, so they like to have everything where they can see it. Consequently, their desks often look cluttered and disorganized and they may even pile paperwork and files across their desk and even onto the floor. A favorite motto of Socializers (usually taped to an almost buried in-basket) reads: "A Clean Desk is the Sign of a Sick Mind."

Their walls usually display awards and displays of their current interests. These might include motivational or upbeat slogans or posters, cartoons, drawings or quotations. You may see reminder notes posted and taped all over the place with little apparent forethought, rhyme or reason. Socializers, if asked, will take great pride to explain to you all the things that are on their desk or on the wall because it gives them a chance to talk about themselves and their interests.

Typically, the preferred decor of the Socializer office would be an open, airy, lively atmosphere that represents the personality of its occupant. Likewise, the furniture arrangement indicates warmth, openness and contact. The Socializer does not like barriers such as a desk to separate him from others when he talks. He prefers comfortable, accessible seating, enabling him to meet his goal of getting to know people better. He might pick the seat next to you at a table or on a couch, so he can see and hear you better and get a feel for the chemistry between you. He talks a lot, with his emotional nature showing in both his body language and speech. Since Socializers are touchers and do not mind a slap on the back or a warm handshake, they often use an alternative seating arrangement to get physically closer to visitors. There is little danger of alienating Socializers by standing too close or picking up something on their desks.

Thinker Environments

When you walk into an office that is free from clutter, neatly organized, and notice that the desk is clear except for one file, a phone and maybe a computer, you are likely to be in Thinker territory. Thinkers like neat, highly organized desks unimpeded by clutter. Everything in the Thinker's office has its rightful place... almost to the point of being preordained. In fact, if you work with a Thinker (and want to have a little fun), wait until they leave their office and then move one thing on their desk. Soon after returning, the Thinker will likely move the object back to its rightful place. However, with prospects and customers, never touch or move anything in the office of the Thinker.

The office walls of Thinkers contain their favorite types of artwork: charts, graphs, exhibits, models, credentials or more formal, job-related pictures.

Thinkers favor a functional decor that enables them to work more efficiently. They tend to keep most resources within reach... readily available whenever needed. However, they tend to keep their materials out of sight and usually locked up to protect their privacy. Where appropriate, you may notice more state-of-the-art technology than with other styles.

Thinkers are non-contact people who prefer the formality of distance. This preference is reflected in the functional arrangement of their desks and chairs, usually with the desks physically separating you from them. They are not natural huggers and touchers, and prefer a controlled handshake and brief visits or phone calls. Although they may not keep eye contact with you, do not interpret this to mean they are not interested in what you may be selling. Unemotional, disengaged behavior is common for those who are "Indirect" and "Guarded."

Relater Environments

Relater's desks contain pictures of family and friends along with other personal items. Their office walls display conservatively framed personal slogans, family or group photos, serene pictures or mementos. They surround themselves with nostalgic memories of stabilizing experiences and relationships. These remembrances of a pleasant, uncomplicated past allow them to transform their offices into a warm, friendly cocoon that shields them from a fast-paced, ever-changing world.

They prefer to arrange seating in a side-by-side, more congenial, cooperative manner... no big, "power desks" for them! If they do have a big desk though, they will usually walk out from behind it to greet their visitors. Colors and furniture selections are generally conventional and conservative in tone.

In addition to family photos and pictures, you may find certificates recognizing the Relater for his volunteer hours for various hands-on activities in the community or business. While other behavioral types may prefer to contribute money, Relaters typically enjoy giving their time for causes they feel strongly about. Not only does this satisfy their need to give, it provides them an opportunity to meet more potential friends and to see what is going on behind the scenes.

In time you will discover that the best way to identify the behavioral style of customers is by looking at their office; it is a reflection of the person who occupies it. For example, when calling upon a customer that is a "managing director" and you see that her office contains a king-sized oaken desk and leather captain's chair along with a slew of trophies, awards, and photos of her standing alongside VIP's adorning the walls, you can conclude you are in the lair of the Director where the weak are often killed and eaten! Just be sure to verify that she was the one who did the decorating before misjudging her style!

Now think about the way in which you have decorated your office? What style would someone guess you are based on the way in which you have decorated it? What about the offices of your boss, co-workers or, if you have children, the way in which they have decorated their rooms? What does their office décor telling you about their behavioral style? Being able to make this determination will enable you to better understand the reason they are the way they are which prompts you to either love them to pieces or drive you absolutely mad!

So take the time now to write up to four things that distinguish the office of each of the four behavioral styles in the table below based on what you read. It will surely enable you to read the behavioral styles of those customers you call upon later and make you a more effective salesperson.

ENVIRONMENTAL CLUES AT A GLANCE:

Relater's Office	Socializer's Office
1.	1.
2.	2.
3.	3.
4.	4.
Thinker's Office	**Director's Office**
1.	1.
2.	2.
3.	3.
4.	4.

Style Identification by Letter, E-mail or Phone

Sometimes you do not get a chance to see your client in person and contact may be limited to an e-mail, phone conversation or a letter. Even these limited communications can offer you clues to the customer's style.

Director's E-mails, Letters and Memos

Director's correspondence tends to be brief and to the point. They may mention highlights of conversations or materials, but they do not detail them unless necessary. They generally include specifics for your follow-through or raise questions they want answers to... *now!* Even notes and cards take on abbreviated forms and with little or no strong feelings and/or tone expressed.

Socializer's E-mails, Letters and Memos

Look for exclamation points, underlining and bold highlighting. If it's an e-mail, you might find unusual fonts, several colors and graphics. In their text, you can almost hear the Socializer emphasizing those emotion-laden, picturesque adjectives and adverbs. Socializers write in the same stimulating, energetic way that they speak. Socializers' letters often include personal anecdotes or references to shared experiences. Socializers are famous for their postscripts and might even include a "P.P.S.: ____"

Thinker's E-mails, Letters and Memos

Thinkers send letters that seek to clarify positions and address processes. Consequently, they may become rather long and filled with information and questions, while at the same time being somewhat indirect and intentionally obtuse. A second type of Thinker letter is a short communiqué with an accompanying host of enclosures, citations or references. The purpose of their letters is to process information in ways that maintain or enhance their position.

Relater's E-mails, Letters and Memos

Relaters send letters to update people or keep in touch and let you know they're thinking of you. Relaters like to send thank you notes for almost anything: inviting them to an office party, bringing lunch back for them or including them on a company function. They may even send a thank you note to acknowledge your thank you note. You can count on holiday season cards from them every year as long as you remain on their "relationship" list.

On the Phone with a Director

Again, the Director prefers to be brief and get right to the point… especially when it's their time or your agenda! They may start the conversation with whatever they are focused on… with no personal acknowledgement or greeting. They often speak in a sort of shorthand – concisely or at least pointedly – and sound cool, confident and demanding. Their phone calls sometimes sound like human telegrams. They tend to speak loudly, rapidly and emphatically… and view phones as task command devices. Because they are not the best at active listening, you may get the sense that they are not hearing what you are saying. However, be sure to measure what you say, as they may later replay the conversation later in their head. Additionally, if something seemed amiss about what you said it could shake their confidence in you and cost you a sale.

On the Phone with a Socializer

"What's up?" "What's happening?" or "How's it going?" are common Socializer opening lines. Their animation and gestures come straight through the phone line as if they're in the room with you. Socializers love the phone and recharge their batteries by talking to others. They speak rapidly with a lot of emphasis and emotion; they can talk longer and better than the other styles. When calling you from a shaky cell phone connection, they may talk for two or three minutes before they even realize the call was dropped. For them, phones are instant "airlines" for transporting them anywhere and anytime for a visit with others.

On the Phone with a Thinker

The Thinker is formal, time-conscious and uses the phone as a tool to process tasks whenever necessary. They prefer brief, to-the-point telephone calls. Thinkers tend to express themselves in a rather tentative manner and display caution in making commitments in phone conversations. Thinkers speak in a careful, soft manner with non-emotional delivery. While the phone does give them the option to avoid face-to-face involvement, they may perceive unscheduled phone calls as an invasion of their privacy, time and/or a disruption from their work.

On the Phone with a Relater

Relaters greet people warmly on the phone, asking, "How are you?" and expressing pleasure at hearing from you. They immediately put you on a first-name basis and patiently listen to your ideas and feelings. Relaters talk more slowly and quietly with a steady, even-tempered delivery. They enjoy listening, since it affords them another avenue to best understand and respond to others; the phone is a valued tool for Relaters.

You have now concluded the first two sections of the book that are designed to help you identify the behavioral style of customers and perhaps others in your life that you may know and love. Thinking to the old adage that "practice makes perfect," it will be well worth the time to fill out the table below to practice the art and science of determining the behavioral style of others using the examples of co-workers, key customers, spouse (significant other), and others. To fill out the table for "Co-Worker 1" for example, think of someone at work who you have contact with on a daily basis. Thinking back on what you read, first determine if that co-worker exhibits direct (D) or indirect (I) behavior and fill in the appropriate circle. Next, determine if that co-worker exhibits open (O) or guarded (G) behavior and fill in the appropriate circle. Now use the results of your assessment to determine if that person is a Director (D+G), Socializer (D+O), Thinker (I+G), or Relater (I+O). Once you have completed the table, you are now well on your way to learning how to adjust the way you sell to the way each of the four behavioral styles prefer to buy throughout the five phases of the buying process that will be presented in Section IV.

Person ___ (DIRECT or INDIRECT) & (OPEN or GUARDED)

	D	I	O	G	Director (D+G)	Socializer (D+O)	Thinker (I+G)	Relater (I+O)
Co-worker 1	O	O	O	O	_____	_____	_____	_____
Co-worker 2	O	O	O	O	_____	_____	_____	_____
Key Cust 1	O	O	O	O	_____	_____	_____	_____
Key Cust 2	O	O	O	O	_____	_____	_____	_____
Key Cust 3	O	O	O	O	_____	_____	_____	_____
Spouse	O	O	O	O	_____	_____	_____	_____
Friend 1	O	O	O	O	_____	_____	_____	_____
Friend 2	O	O	O	O	_____	_____	_____	_____
Others	O	O	O	O	_____	_____	_____	_____

WRAPPING UP...

Environmental clues will help you confirm your style identification of the people around you: clients, co-workers, friends and family. Once you are comfortable that you understand their style, you can begin to communicate with them on their own wavelength ... in their own style. The next section explains two fundamental adjustments you can make to improve your communication with anyone you meet. It also provides you with strategies for improving your effectiveness with your customers at each step of the sales process.

SECTION III

adapting your style
"KNOWLEDGE WITHOUT APPLICATION IS USELESS."

We have all heard that age-old axiom, but it is true. Understanding your natural behavioral style and learning to recognize another person's style is a good start to sales success, but unless you are willing and able to adapt, you have gained nothing. This section will teach you how to make adjustments in your approach to others to reduce tension and engender trust.

6

reducing tension...
through style adaptability

elationship tension is the normal tension that exists between two interacting people. The tension can be either constructive or destructive, but it is always present. Tension is caused by the differences in the way people perceive and manage themselves and others, preferences for closeness and self-disclosure, and other fascinating nuances of personal style. Since you now know that one of the key underlying factors of tension is due to the differences in behavioral styles, this section of the book will help you learn how to adapt your style with each of the four distinct behavioral styles to reduce tension. As a result, you will get along better with others, enjoy more interactions, and increase your sales!

TENSION AND PRODUCTIVITY

The relationship between personal tension and productivity has been the focus of many theories. People function best within a range of tension that has become known as the "comfort zone." If tension is too low, there is little motivation to produce. Conversely, if tension is too high, it turns into counterproductive stress. Between the two extremes is one's comfort zone... the area of optimal productivity. The level of tension that creates this comfort zone is different for everyone.

Everything you do to help your customer stay in his comfort zone enhances your relationship. Everything you do to take him out of that comfort zone erodes the relationship. **Platinum Rule** salespeople are constantly managing the tension level between themselves and the people around them.

PACE AND PRIORITY

Two primary areas of difference that cause of lot of tension and/or static are: *pace* and *priority*. **Pace** is a person's operating speed. Some people prefer a faster, high-energy pace while others prefer to operate more slowly. Priority is what the person sees as most important, their natural inner goal or drive; a natural focus on either the tasks and results or relationships and feelings.

You may remember that a primary quality that distinguishes Direct from Indirect people is their pace. Direct people tend to move, think, talk and make decisions rapidly, whereas Indirect people move more slowly.

Also, another major factor that differentiates Open and Guarded people is their priorities. Open people tend to place a higher priority on relationships while Guarded people view the task as the more important priority. Each style has a unique set of priorities involving the type of relationship or task aspects of a situation that are more important to them, and each has its own pace in terms of how fast things should be done. For some, their expectation is, "I want it yesterday," for others, "sooner or later" is acceptable. The next chapter will help you develop specific strategies for adjusting your pace and priority to meet the needs of other people within all of your relationships.

BEHAVIORAL ADAPTABILITY

The willingness to develop and demonstrate behaviors not necessarily characteristic of your own style, for the benefit of every relationship, is called "behavioral adaptability." This type of flexibility is something applied more to you (to your patterns, attitudes and habits) than to others. Behavioral adaptability involves making intentional adjustments to your methods of communicating and behaving, based on the particular needs of the relationship at a particular moment in time.

Behavioral adaptability is the key to successfully communicating your ideas to people of every style. As you continue to develop more adaptability, you will more effectively interact with each person in the way he or she likes to communicate, learn and make purchases.

Adapting your behavioral style is a big change, and big changes take time. Here is a simple test: move an appliance you use every day (toaster, coffee maker, electric razor, etc...) before going to bed. Quite likely, when you wake up in the morning and go to make toast, coffee or shave, you will automatically go to where the appliance used to be as opposed to its new location. The point we are making is that old habits are hard to break, but breaking some habits is absolutely worth the effort!

It's not easy to break the old habit of "selling the way you buy." You need to learn to sell to people based on their style, which means learning to alter your sales strategies and techniques to fit four different buying styles.

To date, you have been interacting with other people in a way that "works" for you. Feedback from your parents, siblings, relatives, teachers and friends shaped your psyche. You will require practice and focus to "unlearn" reflexive communication modes and to develop new reactions to situations and people.

The beauty of The Platinum Rule is that unlike traditional sales training, you learn more than just "selling techniques." You learn to read the behavioral styles of others and adjust your selling style to one that best fits their buying style. If you are a jokester or storyteller (Socializer), you will learn when and how to use your natural gifts at a more appropriate time to get the results you want. Additionally, you can also learn how to use your agile, creative mind to ask better questions of your customers to gain valuable information and/or cement your relationship.

The first few times you consciously adapt your style to mesh with others, it will feel awkward. Like trying anything new for the first time, it takes practice. However, the day will come when you effortlessly read the style of others and adapt your selling style to match every customer's preferred buying style. Once you begin to unconsciously read and react to the styles of others, this will be the magic moment in time when you begin to benefit from increased sales, and indirectly benefit (which may be even more important) by having a better relationship with your co-workers, colleagues, spouse, children, relatives and friends.

No one style is naturally more adaptable than another is. For a given situation, the appropriate adjustments that people of each behavioral style needs to make will vary. The decision to employ specific behaviors is made on a case-by-case, situational basis. For instance, you may have to be flexible with one person and less flexible with another. You may want to be quite flexible with one person today and less flexible with that same individual tomorrow. Behavioral adaptability concerns the way you manage your communication and action strategies.

For example, when a Socializer meets with a Thinker, one of the ways the Socializer can practice behavioral adaptability is by talking less, listening more and focusing on the key facts. This is not being "phony"; it simply means that the Socializer makes an effort to put the Thinker's priorities ahead of his own, knowing that both their needs will eventually be met.

Adaptability does not mean imitating or "mirroring" the other person's behavioral style. It does mean adjusting your Directness/Indirectness and Openness/Guardedness (your pace and priority) with the other person in ways that lead to synergy and better outcomes for both of you. It means you can make these adjustments while still maintaining your own identity, ideas and good business sense.

Adaptability is important to successful relationships of all kinds. People may display a different style to meet the requirements of their professional roles than they prefer in their social or personal lives. It is interesting to observe that people tend to be more adaptable at work with people we know less; and, by contrast, less adaptable at home with people we know better.

Of course, adaptation at its extreme could make you appear "wishy-washy," or even two-faced... a proverbial jellyfish. A person who maintains high adaptability in all situations would have difficulty coping with stress or realistic requirements for efficiency. There is also the danger of developing tension from the stress of remaining in a "foreign" style permanently... rather than as a temporary, more situational response. At the other end of the continuum, little or no behavioral adaptability will cause others to view someone as a rigid and uncompromising "robot" because they insist on behaving according only to their own natural pace and priority.

High adaptors meet the needs of others (in addition to their own needs). Through attention and practice, they are able to achieve a balance: intentionally using their flexibility by recognizing when a modest accommodation is appropriate, or when the nature of the situation calls for them to adapt totally to the other person's behavioral style. A skilled adaptor knows how to negotiate relationships in a way that allows everyone to win. They are tactful, reasonable, understanding and non-judgmental.

Your adaptive level influences how others judge their relationship with you. When you raise your adaptive level, both trust and credibility will go up; lower your level, and trust and credibility go down. Adaptability enables you to interact more productively with difficult people and helps you to best respond to tense or complex situations. By adapting, you are truly practicing the **Platinum Rule** by treating the other person the way they want to be treated.

TRAITS OF HIGH ADAPTORS

The ability to become skillfully adaptive in our relationships with others requires a diverse set of personal attitudes and strengths... in addition to a well-developed set of mental and emotional abilities.

Higher adaptability may be characterized by the following types of personal attitudes:

- **Confidence:** the attitude of belief in one's self, trusting your own judgment and resourcefulness

- **Tolerance:** open-minded state of acceptance; willingness to defer judgment on the basis of limited time, information, or experiences
- **Empathy:** sensitivity to another's point of view; caring approach towards others (without being overwhelmed or manipulated by people)
- **Positive attitude:** maintaining a state of positive expectations about people and situations, including a positive state of energy in your thoughts and emotional patterns
- **Respect for others:** desire to understand, accept, and consider both mutual and separate interests, choices and commitments
- **Cooperation:** the desire to work with people to develop win-win results
- **Approachable:** open to discussions of events, ideas and feelings with others

The aptitudes that characterize a high adaptor include:

- **Resilience:** learning how to cope in spite of setbacks, barriers, or limited resources; willingness to continue practicing, growing and learning
- **Vision:** foresight, creativity, and imagination
- **Attentiveness:** being mindful and aware of stimuli in the environment; reality-focused to conditions, events, and patterns
- **Competence:** capability of managing required tasks and being knowledgeable about required subjects and people; including use and updating of appropriate abilities
- **Self-correction:** able to initiate and evaluate your own behaviors, seeking feedback as appropriate; characterized by a problem-solving mind-set and approach to matters
- **Objectiveness:** the ability to deal with facts and make decisions on a logical, rational basis
- **Tactfulness:** being able to give people feedback in a kind, gentle manner

The highly adaptive person generally has a solid sense of security and a more fully developed sense of personal worth or well-being. He is open-minded and has a searching attitude in dealing with people and situations. Flexible people generally have positive expectations about both their own goals and desired results, and those of others. They seldom react to people, conditions, or events out of fear or anxiety. Besides, the consummate Platinum Rule sales professional is not one who blindly formulates and adapts a selling style based on salespeople in the past who have been poor role models – aggressive, pushy, fast talking, hard to trust – but instead learns to sell in a way that makes perfect sense.

The good news is that anyone can become more adaptive, but it will take a dedicated, conscious effort to develop the skills. For most of us, flexibility involves learning new techniques and developing new habits. It takes personal commitment to develop the traits and aptitudes necessary for success. It also takes occasional review and feedback to see how well you are doing at developing the adaptive proficiencies you desire.

Although the chapter you just read on reducing tension through style adaptability was a short one, it may be one of the most important in the book because it is in keeping with the Platinum Rule, "Do unto others as they would have you do unto them." Using a baseball analogy, learning to sell the way each of the four behavioral styles prefers to buy will mean less strikeouts at the plate and more base hits to put yourself in a position to score a sale. So before reading on, take a few moments to put our general strategies for adapting to each of the four behavioral styles into your own words so you can apply that knowledge later in the book when we discuss the five steps in the buying process.

7

platinum rule adaptability strategies

HOW TO CONNECT WITH CUSTOMERS, PROSPECTS AND REFERRAL PARTNERS

O nce you understand your own primary style and the style of the person you want to build rapport with, you can begin to adapt your style. Your first adaptations should be *pace* and *priority*. By making simple adjustments in your speed of operation and your focus on tasks or relationships, you can eliminate a lot of relationship "static." Remember that changing your style takes time, practice and patience. Life is a journey; this is not a quick fix. This is why you should refer back to this book often and consider every human interaction a wonderful opportunity to practice raising your level of adaptation.

ADJUSTING YOUR PACE

If you are a Direct person, you tend to operate at a fast rate. If you want to connect with an Indirect person, you will want to talk, walk and make decisions with them more slowly. Seek the opinions of the other person and find ways to acknowledge their ideas. Invite the person to share in the decision-making process and follow their lead rather than trying to take control. Try to relax and be a little more "mellow."

Be sure to engage in active listening to ensure that you thoroughly understand what the other person is saying. Resist your impulses to interrupt; if necessary, jot down one or two-word notes to remind you about your ideas later. Listen more than you talk, and while you are speaking, provide pauses to encourage the other person to speak up. Avoid the impulse to criticize, challenge or push the communication along faster than the other person wants to go. Try to find points of agreement, but if you do disagree, choose your words carefully and do not intimidate the Indirect person.

By contrast, if you are an Indirect person, you tend to operate at a slower speed. If you are dealing with a Direct person, you will want to talk, walk and make decisions with them more rapidly. Initiate conversations and give recommendations. Use direct statements and avoid tentative, roundabout questions. Communicate with a strong, confident voice and maintain eye contact. If you disagree with the Direct person, express your opinion confidently but tactfully. Face the conflict openly without turning the conflict into a personal attack.

ADJUSTING YOUR PRIORITY

If you are an Open person, relationships and feelings primarily motivate you; they are your top priority. If you are dealing with a Guarded person whose top priority is getting things done, you must make a behavioral adjustment. Increase your task-oriented focus by getting right to the agenda. Talk about and focus on the bottom line of the project at hand. The person you are dealing with will want logic and facts, so be prepared to provide proof of your rationale with supporting information.

Consider finding a Guarded associate to help you review your presentation or proposal for logic and flow of information. Prepare an agenda of what items to cover in your meeting and try to stick to that agenda. If you find yourself getting off-track (and this is natural), use the agenda to refocus on the task. When you have completed the agenda, end the meeting on a cordial, businesslike note.

Guarded people do not like to be touched by strangers or to have their physical space invaded. Do not initiate physical contact until you are sure it will be positively received. Downplay your natural enthusiasm and body movement; a Guarded person often views an excess of enthusiasm as "hype." It's much better to have a well thought out, logical presentation based on factual information. Dress and speak in a professional manner compatible with the successful people in your industry. A Guarded person needs to trust and respect you and your credibility.

If you are a Guarded person interacting with an Open person, you will need to remember to develop the relationship first. Share some of your feelings, let your emotions show and let the Open person know who you are and what you like. Observe the other person's environment and find something – a picture, trophy, art object, or something else you have in common – and ask them questions about that object. Try to find out what interests the Open person. Find something about the person or the person's environment that you can sincerely compliment.

Listen to (and respond to) expressions of feelings. Find out what it takes to make the Open person look good within his organization. Take the time to develop a strong relationship based on your understanding of his needs and objectives. Use friendly language and communicate more. Be flexible with your agenda and be willing to address the interests of the Open person… not just your own.

Initiate physical contact and try standing a little closer than your normal style might dictate. Use a few relaxed gestures like leaning back, smiling, or gently patting the other person on the back or shoulder.

GENERAL STRATEGIES BY BEHAVIORAL TYPE

With Directors: Be Efficient and Competent

When adapting your style to a Director, it is important to acknowledge their priorities and objectives. Learn which goals are most important to them and then let them know how you can be an asset for helping them achieve each one. Be professional, competent and businesslike. Get down to business immediately. Be punctual (if not early) to the appointment, have a prepared agenda and stick to it! If you find yourself running late to the meeting, be sure to call ahead and explain the facts behind your reason for tardiness, apologize, and give the Director the option to either move ahead with the meeting as planned or to reschedule. Of course, calling to apologize for tardiness is just common courtesy (regardless of styles), but it is critical to do so with people who place a high value on their time.

If you disagree with them, keep your objections based on facts; not personal feelings. Recognize their ideas and achievements rather than them personally.

Give them options and offer analysis to help them make a decision. Be brief, efficient and thoroughly prepared. Directors want to know what your product or service does, the time involved and what it will cost. They are interested in saving time, results, increasing profitability, forward progress and gaining any edge over competition.

With Socializers: Be Interested in Them

When adapting to a Socializer, support their opinions, ideas and dreams. Find out what they are trying to accomplish and let them know how you can support them. Do not hurry the discussion and allow them to discuss sideline issues or personal interests. Be entertaining, fun and fast moving, but do it without removing the spotlight from them. Allow your animation and enthusiasm to emerge. Take the initiative by introducing yourself in a friendly and informal manner and be open to new topics.

Clarify the specifics of any agreements, in writing if possible, to make sure the Socializer understands exactly what to expect from you and your product or service. Summarize who is to do what, where and when. Minimize arguments and conflict. Use testimonials and incentives to influence the decision process in a positive manner. Illustrate your ideas with stories and emotional descriptions that they can relate to their goals or interests.

Socializers are interested in knowing how your product or service will enhance their status and visibility. They are interested in saving effort, so make the process easy for them. Once they make a decision, they do not want to be bothered with paperwork, installation, training or service problems. Clearly summarize details for them and direct them towards mutually agreeable objectives and action steps that will make things work without being dependent on their follow-up actions for this to occur.

With Thinkers: Be Thorough and Well Prepared

Adapting to a Thinker requires careful, well-prepared support for their organized, thoughtful approach. Greet them cordially, but then proceed quickly to the task without spending time with small talk. Demonstrate your commitment and sincerity through your actions rather than words or promises. Be systematic, precise and provide solid, tangible, factual evidence of the benefit of your product or service. Be prepared to answer the detailed questions that Thinkers ask.

Provide all the critical information and key data required by the Thinker, and also give him summaries and overviews to assist his analysis. Thinkers love charts, graphs and analyses that boil a lot of information down into a concise format. Give them a well-balanced presentation of the advantages and disadvantages of your proposal, including likely consequences. Back your proposal with guarantees that substantially reduce their risk of making a decision to move ahead with your offering. The closer you can come to a risk-free decision, the more likely you are to get an approval decision from a Thinker.

Thinkers want to know how your product or service works and how they can justify it logically. They are risk avoiders; their greatest fear is that they will be embarrassed by a poor decision or action. Provide them with enough data and documentation to prove the value of your proposal. Give them time to think and make their choice; avoid pushing them into a hasty decision.

With Relaters: Be Warm and Sincere

Adapt to Relaters by being personally interested in them. Find out about their background, their family, their interests and share similar information about yourself. Allow them time to develop confidence in you and move along in an informal, slow manner. Encourage them to get other interested parties involved in the decision-making process (since they will anyway).

Assume that they will take everything personally and minimize disagreements and conflict. Practice your active listening skills, be sure to take notes and display your commitment to them and their objectives. Provide guarantees and your personal assurances that any decisions they make will involve a minimum of risk. Let them know how your organization works and how it stands behind your products and services.

Relaters want to know how your product or service will affect their personal circumstances. Save them any possible embarrassment by making sure all the interested parties and decision makers are involved with the sales process from the beginning. Keep the Relater involved and emphasize the human element of your product or service. Communicate with them in a consistent manner on a regular basis.

USING ADAPTABILITY IN MULTI-PERSON MEETINGS

Scott Zimmerman's experience applying adaptive behavior:

After reading Tony's book, "*The Platinum Rule*," I began practicing adapting my behavior around people of other styles. One day, I found myself in a situation that put my training to the ultimate test.

I received a phone call from a business growth consultant who focuses on helping financial planners. He told me that one of his clients was now an ideal prospect for Cyrano (new marketing technology I invented) and that I should call on them. He gave me the name of one of the managing partners, Steve, and wished me luck. Before he hung up, I asked if Steve was more of an extrovert or introvert. The consultant laughed and said that Steve was a closet stand-up comedian and that I would have fun on this sales call.

I called "Steve" (not using real names) and we hit it off immediately. He was funny and quick-witted. At the end of our phone call, I asked

Steve to set up a meeting, so I could "show off" my system in front his partner and the other staff members. We booked an appointment for the following week. Obviously, Steve behaved as a Socializer.

When I entered the boardroom for the presentation, I first met with a marketing manager (Theodore) they had recently hired. "Steve the Socializer" was not yet present, so I chatted with Theodore. He was calm, reserved and spoke with a British accent. We talked about many things (a mix of business and personal topics) until the others began arriving. I guessed Theodore to be a Relater, but possibly a friendly Thinker. I made a mental note to watch him closely during the meeting for more clues.

As Theodore and I were progressing in our conversation, Steve burst in and interrupted. He smiled, pumped my hand and began sharing stories. I have to admit that he was charming and funny, but I could see Theodore was slightly annoyed at Steve's insensitivity to the situation. Bingo! Theodore was a Thinker, because he wanted to steer the conversation back to the business opportunities we had been discussing. Steve's digressions were barely tolerated.

As I started the demonstration of my system, Theodore suggested that Rita sit in. She was the office administrator and would be responsible for helping others use the system, should they decide to buy it. Rita walked in and offered a very soft handshake when I stood to greet her. She actually looked down when I introduced myself. I thought, "She's either a Relater or a Thinker." Either way, I knew I would be taking my time and answering many questions for Rita and Theodore after my formal presentation.

As we sat down, I asked Steve if his partner would be involved in making the final purchasing decision. He initially said "no," but quickly changed his mind. Steve said that he could buy my system on his own, but that Derek (his partner) loves trying out new technologies, if they save time, effort and money. Steve left the boardroom to hunt down Derek. A few seconds later, both returned.

Derek was a classic Director. He strode into the room as if he owned the place, walked right up to me, put out his hand and confidently introduced himself. Ignoring everyone else in the room, he took a seat directly across from me and began asking me pointed questions about myself, my background, my company and the system I had developed. Once I saw that he was convinced that I knew what I was talking about, I looked him square in the eye and said, "Derek, with the talent sitting in this room, this meeting is costing you more per hour than you'll pay to lease my system for an entire month. I'm confident that Steve made a sound decision by inviting me in and that Theodore and Rita will do a thorough job of researching this opportunity before investing one thin dime of your money. Would you agree?"

He nodded, so I followed up with, "If system does exactly what I promise it will do, would you agree that it would be ideal for helping your team cement relationships with your referral partners?" He said "yes." I ended with, "Then you and I both know that this system will pay for itself many times over within six months. The only way you will lose is if your rainmakers don't enter their contacts into my system, and you already hired Theodore to ensure that will never happen. I'm going to cover all the details with Theodore and Rita now, and they will provide you with an overview and their recommendations when we finish up. It was a true privilege meeting you, and I believe I'd be doing Steve and yourself a favor by excusing you both from the details I will be covering during the rest of my presentation."

Steve and Derek stood up, shook my hand and left the room. They had both sold themselves on me within the first five minutes, and I knew it.

I spent two more hours with Theodore and Rita covering the system, step-by-step-by-step-by-step-by-step-by-step. I slowed my pace and covered one point at a time before moving on to the next area. After making each point, I asked a clarifying question to make certain that each understood the benefit before moving on the next idea.

At the end, I gave them an overview of why to use the system, covered the amount of the investment, showed them how the system will be profitable (using their numbers) and I did not ask either of them for a commitment. I knew they would try to shop for alternatives, so I encouraged them to do so. They told me to follow-up with them in two weeks, and I did so.

During those two weeks, I e-mailed them articles I had written, a case study about another company who had grown sales using the system and an excerpt from a best-selling business book that described the need for something similar to Cyrano. On the appointed day, I called Theodore and he gave me the good news: they were my newest client.

Here is an important point: *They were buying me as much as they were buying technology.* By building and maintaining rapport with each person before, during and after the selling process, I made a sale. I simply adjusted my pace and priority with *each person* involved in the buying process.

"Adapt-ability" Works!

In summary, effectively adapting your style meets the key expectations of others in specific situations… whether in personal or business relationships. Through attention and practice, you can achieve higher "adapt-ability" levels and recognize when it is necessary to adapt to the other person's behavioral style.

Practice managing your interaction with customers based on their style and everybody wins. Be tactful, reasonable, understanding and non-judgmental; these behaviors will allow you to engage in deeper conversations that enable you to meet the needs of the other people (as well as your own). The self-knowledge you will gain as you begin to develop higher adaptability in your behavior will help you identify your own strengths and weaknesses. As you gain more understanding, you will be able to avoid potential pitfalls of dealing with diverse people. Over time, you will better understand other people's behaviors and become naturally comfortable in dealing with them more effectively.

As you develop your adaptability to more effectively deal with the other person's expectations and tendencies, you automatically decrease tension and increase trust. This enables you to interact more positively with all people... including customers you may have previously lost due to a conflict in selling/buying styles. You will ease strained situations while establishing rapport and credibility. Your ability to adapt your style will make the difference between harmonious, productive relationships or friction-filled encounters with others.

In this chapter, you read how Scott Zimmerman used adaptability to increase his effectiveness as a salesperson. If you are now in the sales profession, think back to a time when you "hit it off with a customer" and it led to a relatively easy and quick sales transaction. Based on what you read, is it possible that the easy sale was due to the fact that you and that customer shared the same behavioral style? In other words, you sold to that person the way your style likes to buy which was naturally in sync with that of your customer (who shared your style) so you were practicing adaptability at the time without knowing it and you were successful as a result.

Now compare and contrast a relatively easy sale with one that was a failure. Might this have been a case where your behavioral style was different than that of your customer and the pace and priority you used to sell in that instance was out of sync and actually increased, rather than reduced, tension leading to no sale? Are there other bad experiences you have had as a salesperson that cost you a sale perhaps due to lack of adaptability on your part? If you think about this further, could the difference between a month where you blew past your sales goals and one where you fell totally short merely be the luck of the draw in that you encountered more customers with the same behavioral style as yours in the great month and more of those with different styles than yours to make for a bad month? And for those of you who may be reading this book and never professionally sold a thing in your life, think how adaptability will make you a better salesperson when given the chance.

SECTION IV

building and maintaining rapport throughout the 5 phases of the buying process

A s we described earlier in the book, there are five definable stages of the buying-selling cycle. Your ability to recognize these stages and to stay in rapport with prospects during each phase will be critical to converting prospects into customers and customers into long-term advocates.

BUILDING AND MAINTAINING RAPPORT THROUGHOUT THE SELLING CYCLE

There are five definable stages to most every buying cycle. Successfully guiding prospects through each phase will lead to positive outcomes for both of you.

1. Connecting: This is the first critical step that begins the process of learning the style of the customer and adapting your selling style to increase the odds of making a sale. When the prospect learns that the salesperson sincerely has his interests at heart, the rest of the sales process continues without obstacles. Once prospects begin to trust you, they will feel more comfortable about sharing their business goals, challenges and shortcomings. When trust and mutual respect are established, you can begin a process of exploring ways to help them grow and prosper.

2. Exploring: For a salesperson well on their way to mastery of **The Platinum Rule**, discovering the needs and wants of the prospect is a top priority. They explore the prospect's situation for needs, opportunities and ideas about how to help move them toward achieving goals or solving problems.

3. Collaborating: The **Platinum Rule** salesperson gets his customers involved in the process of determining the best product or service solution. They collaborate to find a custom-tailored solution to meet the prospect's needs.

4. Confirming: For the most effective salespeople, gaining a firm commitment from a customer or prospect is often just a formality. When the process of exploring for the right solution has been a joint effort, the final commitment is a natural outcome. Still, this stage is a critical part of cementing the customer-salesperson partnership; *both* parties need to *confirm* specific commitments each are making to the sale and the delivery of the products and/or services.

5. Assuring: Assuring customer satisfaction is the last phase of the sales process, and it is the secret to long-term, extraordinary success in selling. Although many salespeople stop after getting the sales commitment, **Platinum Practitioners** ensure each customer receives the service, training, installation and maintenance that exceed their expectations.

You are now ready to apply what you know about behavioral styles in the context of the sales cycle. As you read this section, we recommend starting with a clean sheet of paper with two columns. The left hand column should list those things you did in the past for each part of the selling cycle before learning **The Platinum Rule**; the right hand column should be the new approach you will develop and implement from this point forward!

In high school or college, you may have used mnemonics to remember lots of information for a quiz or exam. One mnemonic method often used by students is to make up an acronym (e.g., HOMES to remember the five Great Lakes: Huron, Ontario, Michigan, Erie and Superior) to remember a list of words that are not ordinarily related which are comprised of the first letter of each word. Using this memorization technique, an acronym for the 5 phases of the buying process using the first letter from the words that comprise the five phases is CECCA: Connecting, Exploring, Collaborating, Clarifying and Assuring. Based on what you just read, can you now recall the five phases of the buying process by simply looking at that acronym? If not, spend some time associating the words for the five phases of the buying process with the acronym so you will remember them and add that information to your sales mastery tool kit.

phase 1
BUILDING RAPPORT
DURING INITIAL CONTACT (CONNECTING)

The introductory meeting with your prospect is the first critical test. Your understanding of behavioral styles, body language (image), your listening and questioning skills, and your product knowledge will all have an impact on the impression you make in the first few minutes of a meeting. In that short, precious time, you can make or break the sale. In that time, your prospect sizes you up and determines if you are the type of person he would like to do business with.

You can make contact with prospects three ways: Face-to-face, via the telephone, or by letter of introduction. Each makes a different impression and has its advantages and disadvantages. While face-to-face meetings make the strongest impression, they are also the most time consuming and the most costly. Each sales situation dictates a different mix of contact types to maximize effectiveness.

If your first contact is over the telephone, you can still determine their style by listening aggressively. Note their rate of speech, the evenness or variations in tone and their overall demeanor. Also, be aware of how much they try to direct and/or control the conversation. Directors will often come across as impatient, terse and cool. Socializers will interrupt you often, talk more than they listen and seem very animated and persuasive.

Relaters will listen carefully, allow the conversation to drift will not notice the passage of time. Thinkers will also listen well, but will be more formal and less free with your use of their time.

The effectiveness of a contact is based on three criteria: your ability to receive feedback from the client, your ability to adapt to their style, and your ability to reach some degree of resolution. The resolution may not be the "big close," but it may be a commitment to move to the next step in the sales process. Personal contacts provide the best opportunity for feedback: verbal and nonverbal.

The purpose of making contact with your prospect is to begin opening up lines of communication. Professional salespeople know that a solid business association goes beyond the immediate product or service offered. The relationship (and the sale) requires the establishment of credibility and the building of trust. When prospects know you sincerely have their best interests in mind, the rest of the process can continue. Today's buyers are appreciative of professionals who show an interest in them, their business, their goals and their lives.

THE PAYOFFS FOR INCREASING YOUR "ADAPT-ABILITY!"

You may expect four key payoffs for investing efforts at becoming more adaptable in your relationships with others. As you develop your adaptability, you are likely to become more:

1. **Successful:** remember the common bond among successful people is their ability to establish and maintain rapport with people
2. **Effective:** as you are able to develop better working relationships with people, you will dramatically increase your personal productivity
3. **Satisfied:** strong, meaningful relationships add a deeply satisfying aspect to our lives
4. **Fulfilled:** fulfill your dreams and goals with the help and support of those around you

Great listeners make the best salespeople… period. Master the skill of effective listening and every other aspect of your relationships will improve.

As important as listening skills are, it is equally important to communicate the value your products and services provide in a manner that is pleasing for customers of each style. The remainder of this chapter contains ideas and strategies for "connecting" quickly and effectively with people of each style.

COMMUNICATING YOUR INITIAL BENEFIT STATEMENT

Why should a prospect meet with you? He does not know who you are and may not be familiar with your company or your product. You need to be able to convey quickly who you are and how you might be able to help him. Express yourself in a way that shows you are sincerely interested in your prospect and that you have a product or service which may help him meet his objectives and/or solve a problem.

Many initial conversations with prospects are by phone. You call prospects and tell them who you are and what company you represent. That part is automatic; but the next part separates the Platinum Rule salesperson from the pack. Traditional salespeople might launch into a canned pitch to tell the prospect how they can be of service - they start selling.

We wish to offer you a different approach. On your first phone call, do not ask to speak with your prospect (the owner or president, manager, etc…). Instead, ask to speak with someone else in the company. Why would you want to do this? Because another person may provide you with enough information for you to determine your prospect's behavioral style before your call is even connected. Imagine how you will relax knowing that you are about to speak with a Relater, or how empowered you will feel as you increase confidence and get straight to the point with a Director. No matter what style of prospect you find, you should have an appropriate introduction prepared. Here are a few examples of how you might introduce yourself to someone of each style over the telephone:

When introducing yourself to a Director, sound confident and increase your pace while you speak: *Mr. Smith, this is Joe Jones with Acme Computer. I just spoke to a business associate of yours, Ted Stevens. He told me you might be in the market for our training services because they will give your business an edge over the competition and increase your bottom line. When would be a good time to meet with you to discuss how I might help your business secure a distinct advantage over your competitors?*	**When introducing yourself to a Socializer, lean forward, smile into the phone, and ramp up your pace:** *Hi, Mr. Smith, this is Joe Jones with Acme Computer. I just spoke with Ted Stevens, who told me that you might be interested in our training packages because they are fun, innovative and effective. I'd like to swing by next week to meet you. I really think we will be able to help you and your business. Perhaps we could meet over lunch? What's your availability?*
When introducing yourself to a Relater, lean back in your chair, relax, smile and slow down your pace: *Hi, Mr. Smith. This is Joe Jones with Acme Computer. I just spoke with Ted Stevens, and he told me that you'd likely be willing to help me out. I was wondering if we could meet so that I could share some of the ways our training service has helped people just like you develop and enjoy stronger relationships with their customers. Would you be kind enough to meet with me in the next day or two?*	**When introducing yourself to a Thinker, sit straight in your chair, slow your pace, and speak clearly:** *Good morning (afternoon), Mr. Smith. My name is Joe Jones, and I'm with Acme Computer. I just spoke with Ted Stevens, who told me you might be interested in our training services because they will help your office run more efficiently. I would like to meet with you and take 15 minutes of your time to describe six of the specific ways we could help your business. When would be a convenient time for us to meet?*

Re-read the table above that gave you examples on how you might introduce yourself to each style over the phone. Are you able to pick out the words and phrases that are intended for you to adapt to each of the four styles? For example, the words "edge," "competition," and "bottom line" are consistent with the behavioral style of the Director. Now pick out those words that are intended for you to adapt to the Socializer, Relater, and Thinker.

Another benefit of speaking with someone else in the company is that it gives you an "internal reference" or "coach." As you may have noticed in our examples, using the name of a co-worker may put your prospect more at ease. Of course, we want to emphasize that you actually get the "endorsement" of the co-worker before asking to have your call connected. This means that you need to "sell" two people, but the rewards are worth the effort. Every step of your process should be completely "above board" and carried out with the highest level of integrity.

If the company is large enough to have a sales department, Joe could ask the receptionist for the name of their top salesperson. When given the name, Joe asks to be connected. Within seconds, his call goes through to a top-performing salesperson, and Joe immediately introduces himself by saying, "Ted, my name is Joe Jones, and I could really use your help. I have an introductory meeting coming up with your President, Diane Brown, and I have never met her before. I'm a little apprehensive about this meeting and I was wondering if you would be kind enough to answer a few quick questions that I have about Diane? It would really help me out."

The first thing to consider is that most salespeople become great at their profession because they like helping people (Joe asked twice for Ted's help). Secondly, as a rule, salespeople listen and talk for a living. Third, they take and/or return phone calls because it is a core skill of the sales profession. Fourth, they are more prone to giving you some information about their boss because they know how awkward it can be when meeting someone they have not met before, and them wanting to make a favorable impression.

Here are some *types* of questions you might ask the third person to determine your prospect's style:

1. "Is Diane a real 'take charge' kind of boss, or is she more 'easy going?'"
2. "In meetings, does Diane do a lot of the talking, or does she usually sit back and listen to the opinions of other team members?"

3. "Does Diane like to discuss politics, news, weather or family… general chitchat, or is she a 'let's-stick-to-the-business-at-hand' kind of person?"

4. "Would you consider Diane to be a swift decision maker, or does she often weigh many options before proceeding?"

5. "Ted, I greatly appreciate your help. I only have two more questions. My company has recently invented some new marketing technology. Our system automatically sends birthday cards, gifts, product literature and customized e-mails from salespeople to their clients and prospects at appropriate times. Does that sound like something that might help your company grow sales?"

6. "Would it be okay if I mentioned your positive response about our new concept to Diane when I speak with her?"

The answers to the first four questions will give Joe a good snapshot of Diane's behavioral style. He will use this information to introduce himself in a way that connects with Diane (when his call is connected), or he may leave her a specific voice-mail that increases the likelihood of her returning his phone call. Here are some tips for leaving effective voice messages:

Listen to their outgoing message and do exactly what they ask, regardless of the style. If they say, "…leave your name, number, and brief message," then do exactly that. If they say, "…leave your name, number, and a message of any length," then feel free to do that, too. The rule of thumb is not to leave a message that gives away so much information they will be able to make a buying decision for what you are selling before ever speaking with you in person.

After listening to the instructions about the type of message to leave on the answering machine, you might consider leaving the following types of messages (depending on their style). Note: the tone and pace should be the same as when speaking to them in person, as noted earlier in this section.

Voice message for a Director:	Voice message for a Socializer:
Mr. Smith, this is Scott Zimmerman with The Cyrano Group. I just spoke with Ted Stevens. He felt it might be beneficial for us to speak, because I may be able to help your business be more successful than it already is. I will call you again later today, but if you would like to call me, you can reach me at (phone number). I am looking forward to helping your business grow. Thanks.	*Hi, Mr. Smith. This is Scott Zimmerman with The Cyrano Group. I was just chatting with Ted Stevens. When he discovered what my company does to help other companies grow sales, he became excited about our unique way of marketing. He said that you'd get excited when you saw what we have created and he couldn't wait to hear what you had to say. Please give me a call when you get a spare minute, I'm at (phone number). Again, my name is Scott and I'm really looking forward to getting your feedback about this new system.*
Voice message for a Relater:	**Voice message for a Thinker:**
Hi, Mr. Smith. This is Scott Zimmerman with The Cyrano Group. I just spoke with Ted Stevens. The reason for my call is that my company works well with companies that are very similar to yours. We offer a proven system to help you build sales and maintain better relationships with your clients, vendors, employees and prospects. Please return my call at (phone number) to arrange a meeting with me so that we can explore a mutually beneficial business relationship.	*Good morning (afternoon), Mr. Smith. My name is Scott Zimmerman, and I'm with The Cyrano Group. I just spoke with Ted Stevens. Ted told me you are the person responsible for evaluating systems, technologies and methodologies related to inventory control. I would like to schedule a time to meet you and discuss exactly how our business can help your firm become even more efficient in tracking and adjusting inventory levels. I will call you back today at 4:30 to arrange a meeting. If you get this message before 4:30 and would like to call me, I may be reached at (phone number).*

Even if the prospect does not grant an immediate appointment, the Platinum Rule salesperson presents the possibility of help and gives some background as to why he is in a position to give it. He starts to build a relationship. A typical comment would be, "Quite frankly, Mrs. Brooks, there are some people I can help and some I can't. The only way we're going to learn which category you fit into is to spend a few minutes together. We'll talk about what you do and what I do to see if there is a common ground upon which we can do business. If I discover that I can help you in any way, I'll say so and ask you for a little more time to learn even more about your situation. On the other hand, if there does not seem to be a need for my services, I'll tell you so and be on my way."

An initial benefit statement would sound like this: "Mrs. Brooks, I've worked with many banks in the area and have shown them how to increase their bottom-line profits by decreasing their accounts payable expenses. I'd like to spend a few minutes learning about your operation to see if you are another one of those people I can help."

The purpose of the initial benefit statement is to show a prospect (quickly) what the benefits would be to her. This will give them a reason to talk to you. It makes sense to tell your prospects up front rather than wait until you're halfway through the sales process. Most customers, regardless of their behavioral style, are benefit oriented. They may be concerned with cost and interested in features, but their need is always based on the benefits they can gain.

Making Contact with Directors

Directors want to know the bottom line. Just give them enough information to satisfy their need to know about overall performance. They do not want you to waste their time giving them a bolt-by-bolt description of your product, presenting a long list of testimonials from satisfied clients, or getting too chummy with them – always remember that they are Direct and Guarded.

When you write, call, or meet a Director, do it in a formal, business-like manner. Get right to the point. Focus quickly on the task. Refer to bottom line results, increased efficiency, saved time, return on investment, profits, and so on. In other words, tell him what's in it for him.

If you plan to sell something or present a proposal to a Director, take care to be well organized, time-conscious, efficient, and businesslike. As impatient as they are with a slower pace, Directors become especially wary if they are unsure about a person's competence. So, make sure they do not question yours. Remember, Directors do not want to make friends with you; they want to get something out of you if they think you have something to offer. Also, they're usually willing to pay for it, even if they do not let you know this.

Your job is to provide both sufficient information and enough incentive for the Director to meet with you. When you call, you might say, "Some of the ways I thought we would be able to work together are .... Could we spend ten minutes to address those when I call you at a time of your choice?" By planting a seed, you may raise his interest level and the priority of your next call, unless, of course, he just is not interested. Since individuals who fit this type pride themselves in being busy, they dislike granting several meetings. However, if they think that time spent now will save time later, they're likely to explore your proposal. They are very interested in saving time and other "costs."

Making Contact with Socializers

Be an especially attentive listener with Socializers. Give them positive feedback to let them know that you understand and can relate to their visions, ideas and feelings. Remember that they are Direct and Open. When you talk about yourself, remember to use feeling words instead of thinking words. Share your vision of the world in terms of your emotions, opinions, and intuitions. Tell stories about yourself, especially humorous or unusual ones, to win the heart (and sale) of a Socializer. Allow them to feel comfortable by also listening to their stories, even to the point of talking about topics that may stray from the subject.

When you write to or personally meet with a Socializer, give the letter or meeting an upbeat, friendly feeling and faster pace. Do not talk about features, specifics, or performance data. In your initial benefits statement, stress those aspects of your product or service that will give them what they want: status, recognition, excitement, and being one of the first ones to have the newest, most dynamic product or service of its kind.

The first time you call a Socializer, use a more open-ended, friendly approach. Tell him who you are and say something like, "I'd like to come by and show you an exciting, new product that will analyze and organize your accounts and help you become even more of a top performing salesperson."

When you meet a Socializer, try to think (or more specifically, feel) in terms of someone who is running for election. Shake hands firmly, introduce yourself with confidence, and immediately show interest in him personally. Let him set the pace and direction of the conversation. Since Socializers typically enjoy talking about themselves, ask questions about them. Ask them about how they got started in the business... but be prepared for lengthy answers. Plan to have as many meetings as necessary to build the relationship and gather information. After your first visit, you may want to meet for breakfast or lunch. Placing a time limit on those two meals is easier than putting a cap on dinner.

Making Contact with Thinkers

Always remember that Thinkers are Indirect and Guarded. They are precision-oriented people who want to do their jobs in the best possible manner. They also seek confirmation that they are correct, but they won't typically volunteer that need. Going about tasks more slowly so they have enough time to check things out, they dislike rushing or being rushed. They operate on a level that prefers thinking words, not feeling ones, so build your credibility by remembering to think with your head, not your emotions. Focus on their level of understanding about the "what's" and "why's" of your proposal. Make sure you elicit and provide satisfactory answers to their key questions.

Before meeting, provide them with a brief overview of the agenda you will be covering so they know what to expect. Show them logical proof from reliable sources that accurately document your quality, record of accomplishment, and value. Once you have verified your credentials, preferably in writing or with tangible examples, you can establish your product's or service's credentials, too.

Speak slowly. Economize on words. Explain why you are

contacting them. Thinkers don't care much about social interaction (beyond common courtesy and standard pleasantries), so get to the point. Avoid making small talk and speaking about yourself, except to initially establish your credibility. Thinkers tend to be somewhat humble and are naturally suspicious of those who talk themselves up.

Making Contact with Relaters

Relaters, concerned with maintaining stability, want to know step-by-step procedures that are likely to meet their need for details and logical follow through action plans. Organize your presentation: list specifics, show sequences, and provide data. If possible, outline your proposals or materials. Satisfy their need to know the facts but also elicit their personal feelings and emotions by asking for their input on "how to" aspects. If you continually remind yourself that they are Open (but Indirect), they will be a customer for life because you will treat them the way they want to be treated with honesty, sincerity, and personal attentiveness.

Listen patiently to Relaters, projecting your sincere interest in them as individuals. Express your appreciation for their steadiness, dependability, and cooperativeness. Get to know them personally. Present yourself to be non-threatening, pleasant, friendly, but still professional. Develop trust, credibility, and friendship at a relatively slow, informal pace. Communicate with them in a consistent manner on a regular basis… especially at the outset. Thereafter, encourage them to contact you whenever they wish.

Contacts with Relaters are best when soft, pleasant, and specific. Include the human element as well as references to things. Mention the name of the person who referred you. Remember, you may have the best product or service in the world, but if the Relater does not like you, they'll settle for second, or even fourth best, from a salesperson she likes working with.

GENERAL SALES AND SERVICE STRATEGIES

The chart below is only partially completed. Add four things to the list that you should remember to do to connect with each of the four styles. The complete chart is located at the end of the book, on Pages 212 & 213.

Directors	Socializers
• Keep your relationship businesslike • Show you've done your homework • Explore their desired results and time-lines • Give options with cost/benefit summary • • • •	• Let them set the pace & direction of the meeting • Show animation and enthusiasm for their ideas • Summarize all details • Save them complications • • • •
Thinkers	**Relaters**
• Be prepared, so that you can accurately answer their questions • Be willing to research answers to questions you cannot answer on the spot • Avoid too much social talk • Provide logical options with documentation; let them think through ideas before continuing • • • •	• Focus on building trust and credibility before building business • Explore their feelings, current practices and relationship needs • Provide guidance, direction and personal assurances • Practice consistent, predictable service with personal attention • • • •

What happens, however, if you are not able to get to the next stage of the sales process – the exploring customer needs stage? What if the prospect either has no current need for your product/service or is not yet ready or in a position to buy at this time? If this is the case, you need to put this prospect into the "follow-up" mode of contact.

What is your "follow-up reputation" in your business? Is it 'always and promptly'? Or, is it 'usually fairly timely'? Or, could it be 'doubtful it will get done'? The highest performers keep their promises and exceed the expectations of their prospects and clients. Be a bear about this one. It isn't a task to be dreaded; it is an opportunity to be seized. You can set yourself apart with good follow-up skills.

What is the difference between "following up" and "following through"?

If your prospect declines or delays the decision to do business with you, you still have obligations to that person, which requires following up. If they do become your customer, you need to follow through; ensuring that every promise is completely fulfilled.

We discuss following through in detail later on in the "Assuring" chapter. You follow through when receiving good news: the prospect says "Yes!"

So, let's take a look at the bad news first: Poor timing! The prospect learns about the product or service you provide and they simply have no current needs in this area. We contend that if you stay in meaningful contact with each prospect, you will be in the right place at the right time when their situation changes. How to best proceed?

First, the prospect deserves to be sincerely thanked for her time and for giving you an opportunity to exchange information. A hand-written note is always appreciated and sets you apart from a vast majority of salespeople that take shortcuts.

Next, you need to stop and objectively reflect upon the circumstances that caused the prospect to say, "No, thank you." Depending upon the situation, you may have a high likelihood of landing the account sometime down the road.

Here is a list of questions that you should ask yourself when debriefing each sales call:

- Did they decline because I proposed a solution before fully exploring their needs and collaborating solutions with them?
- Did I do my best possible job of asking questions; encouraging them to share their ideas, or did I do too much "presenting" of my ideas and possible solutions?
- Did I adjust to their pace (faster versus slower) and to their priority (task versus relationship)?
- Am I confident that I helped them make the best possible decision that is in their best interests?
- By behaving respectfully and professionally, have I left the door open for doing business later if their situation changes?
- Based on their reasoning for not buying, might the situation change in the future?

True sales masters become comfortable hearing "no", as long as they have gotten to the real reason(s) for the answer.

After careful, objective analysis, you are now fully prepared to follow up with this prospect. We believe that in many cases you can often turn a "no" into a "yes" if you execute customized, long-term follow-up campaigns.

It is common for salespeople to be in the right place (a qualified prospect), but at the wrong time. Many prospects, if empowered to educate themselves over time, can—and often do—change their own minds. However, no one likes to have to do so in front of a salesperson.

There are two different types of follow-ups that you can execute; each serves a specific function.

The first is a standard type of follow-up. The salesperson sends literature, case studies, testimonials and other "value proposition" information designed to further educate the prospect about the value your product/service delivers. Sometimes this does work, but no matter how cleverly disguised, it might convey a message similar to: "You didn't say 'yes' during our discussion, so here's evidence that may help you change your mind."

While this "traditional" practice of marketing is acceptable, it can be improved. Although educating prospects is never a bad idea, "attention erosion[1]" is making it harder to get your messages received, read and digested. Businesspeople today are over-taxed, stretched thin and have little time to spare reading your literature and newsletters.

However, we bring good news: The second type of follow-up makes the first type much more effective...

Dale Carnegie taught us that to get what you want, first help others get what they want. He said that if we live our lives helping others achieve their goals; everything we desire will come back ten-fold. We heartily agree.

"Treat others the way they want to be treated," is our mantra. It's **The Platinum Rule®**. By blending the Carnegie philosophy with ours, then adding a mix of *cutting-edge technology*, we were able to create a new method of following up with everyone in a customized, effective manner that ensures marketing messages are received with open arms (and open minds!).

Goal-specific Communication is the act of sending people (prospects, customers, clients, colleagues, referral partners, etc...) information that helps each of them achieve specific goals or seize a new opportunity.

If you take the time to ask interesting questions and pay careful attention to answers, you can now leverage technology to automate follow-ups that send articles, tips and ideas to each of your contacts that match their goals, challenges, interests and preferences.

Pay careful attention to this statement: If you send people helpful information—especially if it is <u>unrelated</u> to what you sell—you will position yourself as a helpful, thoughtful professional, and not as a pesky, pushy salesperson.

For example: Let's say that Scott is calling on a sales manager and exploring ways to possibly help the sales team develop new skills and create more effective marketing messages. While Scott's company happens to provide solutions in these areas, he also discovers that the prospect is relatively new to his position and has not received formalized management training. Additionally, he learns that they invest large amounts of time, focus and money attending several trade shows.

After the sales call, Scott executes a "blend" of follow-ups for this prospect. Using **The Cyrano Marketing System**, he selects a series of articles written by experts in the areas of interviewing, hiring, managing and interpersonal communications; all containing information that the prospect would find helpful in becoming more successful in his career. These are "relationship building" messages; chosen specifically to help this prospect become a more effective manager. These messages contain no information about Scott, his company or his products; they only serve to help the prospect.

When the prospect receives a few e-mails or articles mailed from Scott, he begins to perceive Scott as someone who is thoughtful, and also as someone who takes action on his ideas. As you might imagine, this type of communication begins building a bridge between Scott and each prospect.

When Scott calls back, he immediately offers to introduce the prospect to one of his colleagues that happens to be an expert in trade show marketing and long-cycle lead conversion. Couple that with the helpful articles on management skills, and Scott has earned the respect of his prospect by adding value at each touch point of the relationship.

More importantly, this approach dramatically increases the odds that when Scott sends "value proposition" information (literature, case studies, etc…) that the prospect will receive each message with an open mind.

By truly helping each prospect, Scott has earned "mind share" with each person. By matching messages to the goals, preferences and interests of every prospect, Scott eliminates "attention erosion". People in Scott's Cyrano database actually anticipate his follow-up messages!

If Scott discovers that the timing is poor with a prospect, he "fills the time" by sending helpful information to him. If the prospect suggests that Scott call back in six months or so, he tells Cyrano what type of articles to send, when he wants them sent, and asks for Cyrano to remind him to call back at the appropriate time. In other words, Scott doesn't get frustrated when he is in the right place at the wrong time. Instead, he simply leverages this to his advantage. By filling the time gaps with showing the prospect that he cares about their success, Scott ensures that when he calls back, his phone calls are eagerly accepted and/or his voice-mails get prompt return calls.

As many thought leaders often remind us: If you want to get everything you want, first help others get what they want!

While conducting our sales training programs, we are often asked if adapting to different styles and/or sending helpful information may be "manipulative."

Our stock answer is, "It depends". If you do it right it is not. If you handle it with a win-lose approach it certainly can be.

If your intention is to help other people; help them make decisions that are in the best interest of their company and/or career (even if it means not buying your product or service), help them achieve more, help them solve problems and help them succeed, then you are in no way practicing any form of manipulation. You are living The Platinum Rule. You are leveraging the power of persuasion in a positive fashion to create win/win outcomes in your business relationships.

However, if your intention is simply to make a sale, mislead another person or do anything that is even 1% less than ethical, then we can confidently state that you are using adaptability, technology and persuasion in a manipulative fashion.

As Malcolm Gladwell pointed out in his best-selling book Blink, almost every person has the innate ability to detect authenticity in another person in mere seconds. As importantly, they do it on a subconscious level; without even knowing they are doing so.

If your intention is pure, prospects and clients will subconsciously be compelled to want to do business with you. Conversely if your intention is to make money, push people into making buying decisions and/or manipulation, then no amount of training, psychology or technology will help you build a long-lasting career in sales.

Here are some important questions you should pose to your sales manager and to your marketing manager:

- Are we effectively leveraging information gleaned from the field (sales calls)?
- Is our contact management system (or CRM) being used to full capacity?
- Are we effectively communicating with everyone in our database?
- Does every one of our prospects know about each product and/or service that we offer, and why they should be buying from us?
- Are we effectively cross-selling to each customer who makes a purchase with our company?
- Should we consider matching our benefits to behavioral styles of our prospects?
- Since it is now possible to automate customized follow-ups (even if salespeople forget), would we grow our sales if we added effective technology to our process?
- Do we have a system for developing leads, cross-selling, increasing customer retention and growing referrals?

These are very important questions for your team to consider.

While it is important for you to learn how to adapt to each prospect or customer during your sales process, it is equally as important for you to market/communicate effectively to ensure that you have a steady stream of qualified prospects, your current customers feel appreciated and thought of often, and you never lose another client due to perceived indifference.

If you hear "No, thank you," or "Not now," from a prospect, they are still a prospect! Regardless if they disengage during the Contact Phase (or any other), staying in meaningful contact with each prospect is a critical component to *Platinum Rule Sales Mastery.*

Let's now assume that you have formed a strong basis for trust and the prospect is willing to openly and honestly share information. It's not time to explore their dreams, visions, goals and challenges.

9

phase 2
MAINTAINING RAPPORT
IN THE EXPLORING STAGE

E ach prospect has a unique situation that needs to be explored before you can make a judgment and recommend a solution. Exploring the prospect's business, needs and opportunities may require research and repeated trips to his office, factory, or home.

Regardless of the behavioral style of any customer, every person you encounter will respond positively to an attentive, patient and intelligent listener. Listening well is a key to exploring, along with excellent questioning skills. The best way to build and maintain rapport with anyone is to ask interesting questions and actively listen to their responses. Unfortunately, many salespeople strive to improve how they present their ideas, but rarely do they learn how to connect with others.

True "connectivity" often occurs *when the other person sees you giving true consideration to their ideas.*

LISTENING AND OUR PERSONAL EFFECTIVENESS

We've all heard people refer to the "power" of listening. Unfortunately, many of us have personal backgrounds or professional experiences that tend to equate listening with "hearing." Because we have the ability to perceive sounds and we can comprehend the words being said, we assume that we have understood and received the speaker's message. We may think of listening as being a natural skill requiring no effort beyond the use of our ears. Many of us invest time and money taking classes and seminars in speaking, writing and reading (the "active" communication skills), but how often are we taught the potent skills of listening?

Actually, effective listening is far from effortless. It is active; and it requires mental processing, hard work and considerable practice. However, the rewards of active listening can be extremely powerful as it provides the listener with an abundance of information and awareness and, when combined with response adaptability, it creates efficient, satisfying and trusting relationships. Effective listening directly supports the Platinum Rule: the listener accurately hears everything the speaker wants to communicate.

Active listening best fits with behavioral adaptability in a given range of varied situations. It is also the most demanding and tiring because it requires the deepest level of concentration, attention and mental (as well as emotional) processing effort.

This most active type of listening refrains from coming to judgment about the speaker's message, instead focusing on understanding her point of view. Be sure to focus on the thoughts, intentions and feelings of the other person, as well as the spoken words. Listening in this manner requires our initial suspension of personal thoughts, feelings and biases. It means (figuratively) "putting yourself into someone else's shoes." It also requires that the listener send verbal and nonverbal feedback to the speaker, indicating that what is being said is really being absorbed and truly understood.

GUIDELINES FOR EFFECTIVE LISTENING

Being a good listener involves applying rules of courtesy and common sense... and more! No one ever intends to be rude, but enthusiasm for a subject or a personal desire to advance our agendas may override courtesy. Similarly, openly participating and contributing to conversations builds common bonds where silence generates doubt and the potential for distrust.

Solid relationships develop over time, and listening plays an important part in that development. The following guidelines for effective listening will increase your proficiency in building customer relationships:

- Listening to the speaker
- Reducing and circumventing communication "noise"
- Preparing to listen and organizing the message you hear
- Checking your listening with the originating source(s)

LISTENING TO THE SPEAKER

Let the speaker talk. Remember that it is impossible to talk and listen at the same time. When an important person speaks, you listen. When practicing the Platinum Rule, the other person is always important. Wait for him to finish speaking and then respond to what has been said. Interrupting someone's comments or injecting rapid-fire statements at the first sign of a pause are possible irritations and may actually slow conversation because the speaker must keep trying to regain his train of thought.

Given the chance to speak uninterrupted, people may reveal interesting facts and provide clues to aid you in helping solve their problems or satisfy their needs. Any interruption could cut short the flow of valuable information. As the speaker reveals needs, you can tailor your response to fit that person's needs, which in most relationships, can also meet your own. Allowing the speaker to talk keeps his attention high and greatly increases the chances of his listening when it is your turn.

REDUCING AND CIRCUMVENTING NOISE

Let the speaker know that you are listening. Face the person squarely with uncrossed arms and legs and lean slightly forward with a relaxed posture. Acknowledge the person's messages with unobtrusive head nods, plus verbal responses, such as "I understand" and "I see." These will never be interpreted as interruptions!

Phrases like, "Tell me more about that," or "Can you give me an example?" or, "Then what?" are referred to as developmental or clarifying probes. Besides providing you with more information, they indicate your attention and invite the speaker to concur, correct, continue or elaborate.

Minimize the impact of distractions. Distractions may be external, such as a ringing telephone or the noise of busy street traffic. Alternatively, distractions may be internal, such as the other person's choice of clothing, their hairstyle, or personal worries about other issues. Try to eliminate or minimize external distractions, and also be aware of, and take control of, internal distractions.

Force yourself to focus your attention on the words, ideas and feelings of the other person, while remaining sensitive to any underlying clues to the speaker's intent. Evaluate the value of the message and respond to it rather than to the person's ability or method of delivering it. Don't let your mind wander off when you hear certain key words, phrases, or references.

While you have no direct control over how the other person may "judge" and respond to your choice of words, your appearance or your accent, being aware of possible reactions will be useful. Ask for feedback to make sure important elements of your message have not been misunderstood (or blocked by internal distractions) by the other person.

Preparing to Listen and Organizing the Message You Hear

Be motivated to listen. Adopt the *proper attitude*, remembering that there is no such thing as an uninteresting speaker, but only a disinterested listener. The acronym **F.E.A.R.** can help you do this. It involves the four types of attitudinal and behavioral adjustment in preparing yourself to listen:

1. **Face:** Face the other person and focus on them with your total attention.
2. **Eye Contact:** Maintain eye contact to reinforce your genuine intention to listen to the other person (be mindful that prolonged

eye contact with a Thinker may be intrusive, so look away occasionally at your notes to keep them at ease).

3. **Atmosphere:** Make sure the climate is conducive to pleasant, uninterrupted and private listening.

4. **Responding:** Verbal and non-verbal (nodding, smiling, etc...) responses build momentum to move your conversation and relationship forward.

Identify the *main themes and key points* in the speaker's message. Use probing questions during pauses or breaks in the discussion to ask yourself, *"What is she really getting at here?"*

Take notes. Do not trust your memory when data and facts are important; use phrases and key words to record the pros and cons of positions, impressions and questions that enter into your mind. Do not attempt to take minutes of the meeting or record complete reactions. Ask the other's permission before taking notes and come prepared with your own pad and pen.

Listen "between the words." What is said may not be what the person means. Learn to read the subtle and not-so-subtle signals that speak so honestly.

Be alert to shifts. Everyone has a unique way of expressing their attitude changes; the words may continue but changes in eye contact, vocal tone, speaking pace, posture, and facial expression may indicate feelings the words are not communicating.

CHECKING YOUR RECEPTION

Offer non-judgmental feedback. Feedback reduces or eliminates "noise" in the communication process (noise: distractions or influences that may be blocking the speaker's real meaning from coming through). Constantly check your understanding of what you hear. Check or monitor the speaker to see if they want to respond or comment on anything you have said.

Although each style has preferences in terms of topics of conversations and how ideas are exchanged, effective listening is a requirement for every behavioral style. Effective listening first requires adjustment and then absolute attention in thought and feeling to the speaker.

While any number of barriers to communication can enter the relationship, communications between some style pairs (Director/ Relater and Thinker/Socializer) tend to succumb more readily to listening tensions than the others. Differences in both pace and priority in these relationships can create significant barriers unless one of the individuals is tuned-in and willing to flexibly respond to the communication style of the other.

NEEDS VS. OPPORTUNITIES

It is important to explore a prospect's situation for problems and opportunities. The only two ways we can help customers with our product or service is if it solves a problem for him or helps him capitalize on a new opportunity.

One important difference between problems (or needs) and opportunities is that needs are the gap between what a customer wants and what he has. This needs gap problem cannot be created... either it exists or it doesn't. However, new opportunities can be created. They are potential sources of new markets, avenues of distribution, promotional vehicles and so on.

For instance, assume you are a computer salesperson talking to a prospect in the advertising business and you find out that his business is slow. The prospect has a computer that he uses to handle his accounting and invoicing so, as fine as it is, he really does not need your computer. But, you continue talking with this prospect and find out that he thinks that one reason his sales are low is because he's not staying in touch with his clients enough; they do not realize all the things he can do for them. You recognize an opportunity and ask him if he's ever thought of doing a newsletter for his customers. You explain how easy it would be for him to design professional-looking newsletters... using the templates that come bundled with your computer's desktop publishing system.

By finding out about your customer's problems and opportunities, you have become a partner to your customer, giving him ideas to help build his business.

Look for opportunities; find niches that your prospect may not have been aware of. Explore your prospect's industry. What are his competitors doing? What trends may be affecting his business now or in the future?

To determine if your product or service will be of any value to your prospect, you must know his current situation, all of its attendant problems, the potential of the business, and his goals and objectives. For example, if your prospect has an unorganized payroll but no desire to be more organized, there is no sense in trying to sell efficiency in the beginning. Note the phrase, "in the beginning." At first, you should accept your prospect's assessment of his situation as valid from his point-of-view or current personal reality. As you develop trust within the relationship, you will be in a position to bring up new ideas that he might not have previously addressed. When you have a strong relationship, you can mention the unorganized payroll and show him a way to save time and money. Having confidence in your expertise at that point, the prospect will be open to your suggestions in creating a future-focused, growing personal reality for him.

One of the primary reasons for the Exploring stage is to give you a picture of the actual conditions surrounding the prospect versus the desired conditions. Often prospects think their goals are being accomplished, when in reality, they are not. They are too close to the situation to see it objectively. After establishing a healthy relationship, it is your responsibility to analyze their situation and point out opportunities they may be missing.

After analyzing a prospect's business, if you find his need gap to be small, then your product or service may offer little or no improvement. In this situation, your advice would be not to buy. When this happens, wrap up the call so you will not waste either your time or the prospect's. You might conclude by saying something like, "Mr. Jones, based on what we've discussed it looks as if I can't offer you a way to improve your sales. If in the next six months, however, you find your sales do not grow by more than 5 percent (or some other condition), we would have a basis for doing business. Do you mind if I keep in touch to see how your sales are progressing?"

When you terminate a call in this manner, your prospect will remain open to future contacts because you did not try to sell him something he did not need. You have planted seeds of good will and trust, which will reap future benefits. Place that prospect's name on a follow-up list and call in six months. When you reach the prospect, ask how things are in general and then ask questions to see if those specific conditions have changed. If they have not changed, ask if you can call back again in six months. If they have changed, get together and review the situation again. At this point, you will already have established trust – a huge asset – and you will be able to pick up from where you left off.

In the majority of cases, after analyzing your prospect's need gap, you will often find that you can be of service.

EXPLORATION TOOL: SMART QUESTIONS

The purpose of Exploring is to get information; an accurate picture of the customer's needs and what it will take to provide an effective solution. To do so, we need to listen to what the customer says, but we also need to know how to ask the right questions to get the information we need.

Asking intelligent questions is a critical sales skill. It does not require asking many questions - just the right ones. The art of questioning is the cornerstone of exploring the customer's needs. It is paramount to a successful career in sales. Asking questions is similar to painting a picture. We start with a blank canvas and begin to fill in the background and rough in the picture with broad-brush strokes. Then we fill in the details using finer and finer strokes.

With questioning, we start with broad strokes asking the customer broad, open questions that rough in a lot of his situation. "Tell me about your business," not only starts to give you information about your prospect's situation, it gives him a chance to relax and tell you what he thinks is important. If you start with a smaller brush, "What was your sales level last year?" that's an okay question, but sales may not be what your prospect's primary concern right now.

Broad, open-ended questions show your interest in the prospect's situation. They often start with "Tell me ...," "how," "what," "why." "How do you see a computer system fitting into your situation?" "What would you like a computer to do for you?" "Why are you looking at computer systems right now?" They are much more powerful than closed-ended questions that require a simple answer such as yes or no or a specific piece of information.

THE FUNNEL TECHNIQUE

Of course, we will use closed questions when we need specific decisions or answers such as "How many people will be using the system?" It is important to understand when to use each type. Once you have started the questioning process, you want to build the responses you have received. You are following the lead of your prospect.

This is commonly referred to as a "funnel" or "channeling" technique of questioning... you start with broad, open questions such as, "Tell me about your business."

Keep in mind that your opening question will be very important in creating a good impression with your prospect. For this reason, you need to size him up as quickly as possible so that the first question matches his style. There are major benefits to asking such a broad question as, "Could you tell me a little about your business?" A question like that gives your prospect complete freedom to answer in any way he chooses. This has a relaxing effect. It also reveals to you his behavioral style, the knowledge of which will help you shape your subsequent questions. Lastly, the answer to this question may reveal needs and opportunities. If it does not, they will become apparent as you build subsequent questions around this answer.

Build on previous responses.

The easiest and most effective way to build a conversation around someone's responses is to take the operative word in the sentence or sentences and create a question based on it. A simple example will clarify this. Imagine two people meeting on an airplane:

"Hello, my name is Ellen, what do you do for a living?"

"I'm a writer."

"A writer," Ellen continues. "What kind of writing do you do?"

"Mostly humor. Occasionally, I write something serious or philosophical, but people often laugh at that, too."

"That's very interesting," Ellen says. "I don't know a thing about writing, especially humor. Tell me about it."

"Well, you take one part sarcasm, add two parts irreverence and one part creativity, shake violently, and hope it doesn't blow up in your face."

In a business context, using the operative word or words would look something like this:

"Could you tell me a little about your business?"

"I'm a distributor of sporting equipment to colleges and universities."

"That's interesting. What kind of sporting equipment?"

"Everything found inside a gymnasium. We don't get into the larger things like bleachers, goal posts, and football fields."

"What colleges and universities do you sell to?" (This plays off the second operative word in the original answer.)

"We sell to every school west of the Mississippi with more than 5,000 students."

"Is there a reason you confine your business to schools west of the Mississippi?"

"Yes, they're easier to reach for service."

... and so on. You get the idea. This technique quickly and effectively works in both social and business situations. There is a built-in, logical order to this method of questioning, and it shows the prospect that you are listening and following along.

Questions should move at a pace that is comfortable for the prospect. He may be hesitant to provide information that is either sensitive or threatening. An inexperienced salesperson who is convinced that his product or service is right for the customer may leap to the question of budget (before the customer decides he or she wants to spend anything at all), thereby risking the possibility of killing the sale prematurely.

There will be many times when you may have to ask a sensitive question. When the need arises, be sure to tell the customer the reason for your question. For example, while opening a new savings account, the new accounts officer may ask, "What's your mother's maiden name?" That may sound personal or odd and put you on the defensive. However, if it were explained that this is for your protection, and that their tellers will ask for your mother's maiden name anytime someone tries to cash a check for over $500 against your account, then you would feel more comfortable sharing such sensitive information.

Questions are the basis of your information gathering activities but it is also important to understand the three primary directions for questions. They are:

1) **Expand:** When you want more information or background data about a certain area, we ask an expansion question. You are trying to get a broader picture: "Tell me more about that..." "How would that work?" "What would that mean to you?"

For example, a woman sees an ad, and calls a landscaper to quote the design and installation of a rock garden. After arriving and establishing rapport (connecting), the landscaper asks "expanding" questions. The

landscaper gets her to describe her vision for a perfect rock garden. "How would it look from your window?" "How prominent would the garden be in relation to the rest of the property?" "What types of things would be in your rock garden?" She begins opening up and sharing her dreams to the landscaper.

2) Clarify: These are questions we ask when we need more details or when we need to verify a perspective or point-of-view. We are focusing in on a single issue: "I'm not quite sure I understand..." "Can you give me an example?" "Do you mean..."

Returning to our example...

By asking some "clarifying" questions, the landscaper discovers that she speaks about flowers more often than rocks. By refocusing his questions on flowers, he learns that she is an avid nature photographer. She immediately pulls down a photo album containing pictures she has taken; revealing him shot after shot of ... butterflies! What she really wants is photo opportunities... and flowers that attract butterflies would be ideal!

3) Redirect: When you want to build on a person's position or change directions, you acknowledge the current issue and then ask question that brings up a new issue. "Okay I think I understand what you think (feel) you need here; what if you could also have ..."

In our example, the landscaper might respond with, "If I've heard you correctly, you would love a garden that attracts exotic butterflies. I happen to have written a published article about horticulture's role in landscape design. If you like, I will call my secretary and have her send you a copy... my gift to you. The article contains a section focused on flowers that produce pollen; the very nectar that attracts butterflies. By the way, how might someone's knowledge about flowers influence your decision in hiring your landscape designer?"

What a great "redirecting" question! You can see how close he is to landing a new client... the mutual bond is forming.

"Direction" questions (expand, clarify and redirect) help us steer through the Exploring process. A skillful salesperson uses this stage to guide the prospect to tell him what he needs to know in order to provide an appropriate, effective solution.

Exploring with Directors

To head off the Director's impatience before it surfaces, keep your conversations interesting by alternately asking questions and offering relevant information. Do this in a practical manner. Directors need to view the meeting as purposeful, so they want to understand where your questions ultimately lead. When asking Director questions, it is essential to fine-tune and make them as practical and logical as possible. Aim questions at the heart of the issue and ask them in a straightforward manner. Only request information which is unavailable elsewhere.

When gathering information, ask questions showing you have done your homework about their desired results and current efforts. Know the Director's industry and his company. Be sure to make queries that allow him to talk about his business goals. Gear your exploration toward saving the Director time and energy.

Exploring with Socializers

Interacting Socializers get bored quickly when they're not talking about themselves. That's why so much information gathering needs to revolve around them. But remember to strike a balance between listening to their life's stories and gathering the information you need to be an effective sales consultant. When asking business questions, keep them brief. If you can, work these exploratory questions in with social questions. You might ask, "You mentioned people as one of the keys to your success. How do you locate (recruit) the people you work with? What kind of training do you give them?" The better your relationship with a Socializer is, the more willing he'll be to cooperate and talk about the task at hand.

Socializers can be so open they may tell you their fondest hopes and aspirations. If you can demonstrate how your product or service can get them closer to their dreams, they may become so excited about your product -- and you -- that they're likely to sell you and your products and services to everyone else in their organization.

Exploring with Thinkers

Thinkers often like to answer questions that reveal their expertise, so they can be very good interviewees. As long as you ask logical, fact-oriented, relevant questions, they will enjoy speaking with you. Phrase your questions to help them give you the right information. Ask open and closed questions that investigate their knowledge, systems, objectives and objections. Ask questions that demonstrate your understanding of the industry and situation. And, most of all, invite them to state the questions -- including any key reservations -- they may have so that you both can discover whether a logical basis for doing business together exists.

Make your own answers short and crisp. If you do not know the answer to something, do not fake it. Tell them you'll get the answer for them by a certain time, and then do it.

Exploring with Relaters

Relaters can be excellent interviewees. Talk warmly and informally and ask gentle, open questions that draw them out (especially around sensitive areas). Show tact and sincerity in exploring their needs.

If they do not have a good feeling about your product, company, or even you, they are not likely to take the chance of hurting your feelings by telling you so. They want to avoid confrontations, even minor ones. So Relaters may tell you what they think you want to hear, rather than what they really think. This same reticence may apply to telling you about their dissatisfaction with your competitors. Even though this is exactly what you want to hear, the Relater may be hesitant about saying anything negative about them.

On pages 155 & 156 we presented the different methods by which to navigate the exploring phase with the four behavioral styles. Before reading on to the next chapter, take a moment or two to develop a five question sequence that could be asked of the four styles using the funnel technique to help you to be effective in the exploring phase of the buying cycle. Case in point, would the first question you posed to a Director in the exploring phase be a casual personal question? If not, which of the four styles would respond positively to such a question? Learning to develop a different set of exploring questions for each of the styles will truly separate you from the rest of the traditional salespeople and move you closer to a sale so give it some thought.

10

phase 3
Maintaining Rapport
in the Collaborating Stage

I n the Exploring phase of the sale, you uncovered your prospect's needs and opportunities and the two of you agreed upon the problems to be addressed. In this phase, you and your prospect Collaborate to find a solution that meets the prospect's needs. It is a process of taking your prospect's ideas and combining them with your ideas to arrive at a solution that makes sense to both of you. The Platinum Rule salesperson keeps the prospect involved at every stage of the sales process in a give-and-take exchange.

Switching Heads

The give-and-take exchange can be thought of as an opportunity to "switch heads" with your prospect. Imagine saying this to your customer: "If you and I could switch heads, that is, if you could know what I know about my product and if I could know what you know about your business, we would both know exactly how to give you the best possible solution for your needs." That's your goal, to come as close as possible to the perfect knowledge that would allow you to develop the ideal solution for your client. To achieve that goal, you need to exchange enough information to fully understand your client's business, industry, trends and challenges; and they have to know as much as possible about your products and services and how they can help them.

The primary roadblock to such a thorough exchange of information is time. There simply is not enough of it. So keep in mind the "three T's" of information exchange: Time, Trust, and Tension. If you decrease tension and build trust, the prospect will want to spend more time with you.

The goal of the collaboration stage is to match a customized package of solutions to a specific package of your prospect's needs. As you propose a solution, relate it to the success criteria agreed upon in the Explore phase and explain how it will work in your customer's environment. Because constant change seems to be our only unchanging condition, at the beginning of each meeting, you should review points agreed upon in the last meeting and get feedback to be sure your prospect is still in agreement.

The Platinum Rule salesperson does not depend on slick, razzle-dazzle presentations and approaches. Instead, they caringly explore the customer's situation for needs and opportunities and then involve the customer in the development of solutions.

SPEAKING THE LANGUAGE OF BENEFITS

In addition to knowing what style language to speak to his prospects, the Platinum Rule salesperson knows how to speak the language of benefits rather than features. A feature is some aspect of the whole product that exists regardless of a customer's needs. A benefit is the way that feature satisfies a customer need. A benefit is a feature in action.

Most customers think in terms of benefits. They do not care how something works; they want to know what it will do for them, or how it will solve their problems. The bottom-line benefit is what the key decision maker looks for. Therefore, the language that will capture their attention is benefits.

One way to get a prospect involved in the collaboration stage is to use the feature-feedback-benefit (FFB) method. A feature is presented with a question that asks for the prospect's feedback. For instance a telephone system salesperson might tell say, "This system can expand to up to 200 lines. How important is that expansion capability to you and your company?" That opens up a lot of discussion about the company, its potential growth, and goals. If the prospect indicates that this particular benefit is very important to them, you can expand your explanation and discussion of the benefit. If it is not an important benefit, you can go on to the next feature until you find the prospect's "hot buttons."

Other questions that are effective during this stage are:

"How do you see this fitting into your situation?"

"What other advantages do you see in this?"

"How do you see this addressing the opportunity we discussed earlier?"

"Does this look as if it will meet your needs?"

COLLABORATING WITH DIRECTORS

Your presentation, whether it is combined with the exploration stage or given on its own, must be geared toward the Director's priorities. They are concerned with saving time, generating results, and making life easier and more efficient. If you gear your presentation toward how they can become more successful, you'll get and keep their attention. Zero in on the bottom line with quick benefit statements.

Because of their lack of time, Directors do not focus as much energy contemplating and evaluating ideas. They want you to do the analysis and lay it out for them to approve or disapprove. Directors like rapid, concise analyses of their needs and your solutions.

So, how can a salesperson get into a better business relationship with a Director? Act like a Boy Scout and "be prepared." In addition, demonstrate your competence and show them how your product will help them achieve their goals. Focus on results and highlight important specifics. Cut out intermediate steps when you make your presentation, eliminate the small talk, and stick to business. Professionalism counts with Directors.

When it is appropriate to give historical data about your company (or a more detailed presentation), write out your information before the call. This allows you to highlight key points in your notes. Otherwise, you may bury them in a mass of paperwork, and fumbling around in front of a Director is a major mistake. Skip over less important facts and show him the bottom line basics. Then leave a copy of the printout so they can refresh their memory later. Additionally, they may want to delegate the fact checking to someone who really enjoys it... a Thinker or a Relater.

Another good reason for reviewing your material, printing it out, and highlighting it is that a Director may fire off questions at what seems to be a faster-than-the-speed-of-mouth rate. When they want to hear about how your product ties into the bottom line, they want to know now. Determine if they really need the information immediately to make their decision or if they just want to challenge you. In many cases, if they you get them the information later, you can still meet their needs.

Directors are very big on their own sense of being in control, so give them choices backed with enough data and analysis to allow them to make an intelligent decision. *Then, be quiet and let them make the decision. If you speak or interrupt while they are buying, you will dramatically decrease the odds of making this sale.*

COLLABORATING WITH SOCIALIZERS

Style is as important as substance to Socializers, so you'd better remember the sizzle if you expect to sell the steak. Your presentation should show how your product or service would increase the Socializer's prestige, image, or recognition. Talk about the favorable impact or consequences your suggestions will have in making their working relationships more enjoyable. Give them incentives for completing tasks by stressing how their contribution will benefit others and evoke positive responses from them. Presentations need impact for people with short attention spans, so involve as many senses as possible. Socializers want both the presentation and the product to feel great. They also want to be reminded of who else has it; but spare them the details of other people's successes. Show them how you can save them effort and still make them look good.

Back up your claims with testimonials from well-known people or high-profile corporations. Socializers respond well to other people's positive experiences with your product or service -- so tell them who else uses it. If one of their heroes believes in something, they are likely to want it, too. Better yet, name some satisfied acquaintances that the Socializer knows and admires. They may even interrupt you by saying, "Go no further. If it's good enough for Fred Mullens, it's good enough for me. He probably spent weeks researching, comparing, and contrasting products. He really knows what he's doing. I'm sold, and you should put Fred on your payroll."

COLLABORATING WITH THINKERS

Emphasize logic, accuracy, value, quality, and reliability when collaborating with Thinkers. Present obvious disadvantages openly. Make your points, and then ask if they want further clarification. They dislike talk that isn't backed up with both supporting evidence and achievement-focused action. Describe the process that you plan to follow. Then outline how that process will produce the results they seek. Elicit specific feedback by asking, "So far, what are your reactions? Do you have any reservations that you'd like me to clear up?" They probably do, so encourage communication with a question such as, "Specifically, how do you view the practicality of applying this computer program to satisfy your current requirements?"

Show thinkers how your product will prove to their company that they are right in the way they do their jobs. They pride themselves on the accuracy of their analyses. Present your product or service in a way that shows them they will be correct in making the purchase. Base your claims on facts, specifications, and data that relate specifically to their need gaps. For example, point out cost-benefit analyses, maintenance costs, reliability data, tax advantages, statistics on increased efficiency, and so on. When you talk about prices, relate them to the specific benefits.

Thinkers are very cost-conscious; therefore, you have to increase their perceived value with facts and return-on-investment data.

Of all the types, Thinkers are the most likely to see the drawbacks, so point out the potential negatives before they do. Such honesty will only enhance your credibility. If you do not draw attention to the disadvantages, the Thinker may view your failure to do so as a cover-up. Instead, let them assess the relative costs-versus-benefits, which are typical trade-offs when making realistic choices between available, competing (yet imperfect) products or services. Ask to review their evaluation with them in search of common understanding.

Collaborating with Relaters

Show how your product or service will stabilize, simplify, or support the Relater's procedures and relationships. Clearly define their roles and goals in your suggestions, and include specific expectations of them in your plan. Present new ideas or variations from their current routines in a non-threatening way. Provide them with the time and opportunities to adjust to changes in operating procedures and relationships. When change becomes necessary, tell them why. Explain how long the changes will take and any interim alterations of the current conditions. Design your message to impart a sense of stability and security. Relaters need to be reassured with comments such as, "This plan will enable you to continue doing things the same basic way, with a few updates here and there. Don't worry about the updates, because I'll be here to walk you through them each step of the way just like I've done with our many satisfied customers. And the real benefit, in the final analysis, is that this refinement will result in a smoother, easier operation."

Concentrate on security, harmony, steadiness, and concrete benefits with statements like, "This pension plan could help your entire staff save for their retirement with a minimum amount of worry. Even though Social Security may be tapped out by the time they retire, they'll be able to depend on this safety net." Answer their concerns about how and what as well as you can. Reassure them that you'll find out about the information they want to know; then do it. Stress that this isn't a big change, just a way to help them do what they already do ... only better.

Relaters like to be shown the appropriate steps to follow, so share those with them. Involve them by asking their opinions. A question such as, "Is this an important concern for you, or are you looking for some other specific critical benefit?" will encourage them to give you feedback about their decision criteria.

Although this chapter on the collaborating phase was short it does not diminish its importance to *The Platinum Rule for Sales Mastery*. To help you remember the tips given on how to successfully navigate this stage of the buying cycle, see if you can recall three tips you were given to collaborate with a Director, Socializer, Thinker, and Relater. Doing so will ultimately make a difference in your bank account so it worth the time to do that before reading further.

11

phase 4
MAINTAINING RAPPORT
IN THE CONFIRMING STAGE

Gaining the customer's commitment flows naturally out of the Exploring and Collaborating stages for the Platinum Rule salesperson. If you did a good job during the first three stages of selling: Contacting, Exploring and Collaborating, the sale should close itself. In fact, a study by Forum Corporation showed that the top sales professionals – the superstars – seldom use a close. During 46% of their sales, they never had to ask for a commitment. When they do ask, it is usually no more than a nudge, something like, "Let's do it," or "Any reason why we shouldn't move forward?"

Top salespeople stay in sync with their customers, taking things one-step-at-a-time. When they get to the end of the process together, signing the order is a mere formality. However, gaining true commitment from your client should not be as simple as closing the deal and signing the paperwork. A top producer's focus is always on making a customer, not just a making a sale.

The Confirming stage is a critical point in building a customer partnership. Top salespeople know how to use acceptance, rejection, or even postponement to develop stronger ties with their customers. Platinum Rule salespeople never use the "puppy dog" close, the trial close, or any other fancy closing techniques. The sales method they use is a very natural process of two (or more) people sharing information to develop a solution to a problem or need. It requires trust, respect and open communication on both sides. You cannot work through all the stages of the sale and then at the end, try to use a manipulative closing technique to clinch the deal. It does not make sense... and it most certainly does not work.

In traditional selling, the salesperson asks "closed" questions frequently meant to force the prospect to say "yes," such as the forced-choice close, the sharp angle close, closing on the final objection, or the "I want to think it over" close. Here is where the salesperson really tries to take total control of the sales situation and the customer. However, this is where the customer really has the strongest need to gain what they want (and can best do so by retaining their inherent right to make this decision without being railroaded into a decision by the salesperson) even if it was the decision they were already going to make. This creates problems in the sales relationship. Often, the prospect may create smokescreens as a defense mechanism to ward off the salesperson.

A smokescreen is something that retards the relationship or obscures the decision-making process. Common smokescreens are "Your price is too high," and "I want to think about it." Both indicate that the prospect is uncomfortable communicating their uncertainty; they are avoiding telling you their true feelings and thoughts. What they are *not* telling you are their true concerns.

DEALING WITH CUSTOMER CONCERNS

In the traditional sales training model, salespeople learn techniques to help them overcome objections. Nothing is more frustrating than to work hard exploring a prospect's needs and collaborating on creative solutions to their problems only to have them come up with a last minute objection.

The first thing a Platinum Rule salesperson does is change the terminology. They drop the word "objections" and call them "customer concerns." Talking about objections makes it sound like the customer is being difficult. They are not being difficult; they are expressing their concerns about the solution you have proposed.

The best way to end the "objection" game is to avoid it in the first place. If you do enough information gathering at the beginning of your sales relationship, and collaborate with your prospect on a solution, there should little left to object to.

If your client has a valid concern that proves that your solution is not right for them, you both will be better off discovering this before or during the sale, rather than after the deed is done. We should actually welcome it when a customer expresses their concerns because they are giving us information to guide us.

Part of dealing with concerns is to move past the discouragement that comes with them and actually welcome the opportunity they provide you to better understand your client's needs. Rather than being rejections, these concerns are course corrections. Clients are often reluctant to express their real concerns up-front... sometimes they do not even realize what their concerns are. Therefore, when they do express their concern, it gives you a chance to make sure you have the right solution that matches their needs.

View customer concerns as an opportunity, not a roadblock.

Here are four steps to help you effectively deal with customer concerns:

1. **LISTEN:** Hear the customer out. Listen carefully for clues to help you reveal their real concern. Sometimes salespeople blow sales just by trying to jump in too soon and overcome an objection. Remember to hear out the concern completely prior to responding.

2. **CLARIFY:** Ask questions to make sure you have a complete understanding of the concern *from the customer's point of view.* What do they mean when they say the price is too high, they

need to think about it, or they need to talk to a friend?

3. **RESPOND:** Respond appropriately to the concern. Refer back to the decision criteria you established in the Explore stage and make sure that each point is still valid. Review the benefits of your product to see where each criterion applies and where your product may fall short.

4. **CONFIRM:** Make sure the customer understands your response and is satisfied with it. Did it really answer his concern? You want to make sure that this same concern does not come up again.

The way we respond to our customer's concerns depends on the **type** of customer concern and the selling stage. Each stage of the sales process has different types of typical concerns. In the beginning, most are simply "put-offs." The prospect is trying to avoid dealing with the salesperson. In the later stages, the concerns most salespeople meet relate to product, price, postponement and personal style.

It is extremely important to handle personal style conflicts immediately. Reading the style of, and adapting to the styles of each customer are the foundations upon which everything else builds. If the relationship collapses, so does everything it supports. This happens because trust was broken; your sales style may not have been appropriate for the prospect or the prospect may not feel that you have a sincere interest in his goals. Somehow, you have lost the confidence of your prospect.

The best way to deal with the problem of "lost confidence" is to avoid it in the first place. If you are sincerely trying to help your clients, not sell them, they will never lose confidence in you. You have to listen more than you talk, always monitor how well you are relating with the customer, and do what you say you are going to do when you say you are going to do it. When there are problems or glitches… fix them and "make things right." Keep on top of your clients' changing needs, so you can alter your plans and policies as needed.

Whatever the cause for the style mismatch, you need to use all of your communication skills to get the relationship back on track.

You should review the prospect's style and make every effort to treat them appropriately.

CONFIRMING COMMITMENTS WITH DIRECTORS

With Directors, you can come right out and ask if they are interested. You might say, "Based on what we've just discussed, are you interested in starting our service or carrying our product?" A Director will often tell you "yes" or "no" (in no uncertain terms). At times, though, this type can put you off as if they cannot make a decision, when, in fact, they aren't even thinking about it. They can become so preoccupied with other business that they literally do not have the time to evaluate your ideas, especially if they do not have enough information. You can easily lose the attention and/or interest of a Director by presenting your information too slowly or by spending too much time discussing details.

When you draw up a commitment letter, be careful not to spend too much time on points the Director may not care about. Explain your commitment to attain both their bottom line results and your goals for a mutually acceptable agreement.

Consequently, the best way to deal with a Director is to present them with options and probable outcomes. Bear in mind that the Director likes to balance quality with cost considerations, so include this information when you want them to make a decision. Offer options with supporting evidence and leave the final decision to them. Directors seek control, so let them make the final decision. Brief, and to the point, like the Director himself, this approach automatically fills his need to have the final word.

We have found that it is effective to present a Director with two or three options. Provide a short summation of each option, along with your recommendation of each.

While the Director is reviewing your proposal, do not interrupt them. The odds are very high that they will find an option that appeals to them and will circle or initial it… closing the deal themselves.

CONFIRMING COMMITMENTS WITH THE SOCIALIZER

Be open and ask, "Where do we go from here?" or "What's our next step?" If your inventory is low, tell them. "I see you really are excited about this, I only have three left. Do you want one now?" Socializers are very spontaneous and respond well to the bandwagon approach of "Everybody's doing it." If they like something, they buy it on the spot (all other things being equal). You may have to hold them back because they also tend to overbuy and/or buy before weighing all the ramifications; behaviors that both of you may live to regret.

Socializers dislike paperwork and details so they are likely to hesitate, and even procrastinate, when it comes to spending the time required on a contract or purchase order. While a handshake is usually good enough for them, you would be wise to have a written agreement prepared due to their tendency to be unclear about business details such as procedures, responsibilities and expectations. Both of you may hear the same words, but Socializers (being optimistic people) tend to color those words in a positive light... and often to their advantage. For this reason, it may help to draw up a summary in advance and go over it with this style of prospect. Make sure that you agree on the specifics or, later on, you can almost bet on some degree of misunderstanding and disappointment.

When the Socializer tells you a written agreement is not necessary, simply say that you need such a clear summary as a crutch for yourself... to help you remember everything you have promised. Also, mention that you appreciate their show of faith in you. When you put your concerns in terms of such desired positive feelings, how can the Socializer possibly object?

CONFIRMING COMMITMENTS WITH THINKERS

Provide logical options with appropriate documentation to the Thinker. Give them enough time and sufficient data for them to analyze their options. They are uncomfortable with snap decisions and when they say they will think about it, they typically mean exactly that! However, if pressured by people or excessive demands, they may use

"I'll think about it," as a stalling tactic in coping with such stress.

Unless Thinkers have already researched the field and determined that your product is the best, they probably have your competitors calling on them. Thinkers are driven, educated, non-emotional "shoppers." Know your competition so you can point out your advantages relative to what they offer. Thinkers are the most likely to do their own comparative shopping, so mention your company's strengths as you suggest questions they may want to ask your competitors. Point out the things your company does better than your competition. Do this in a factual, professional way that allows them to do a comparative cost-benefit analysis of the options. In addition, be willing to explore the subject of a conditional, "pilot program" as a way of reducing their risk. This provides you the opportunity to demonstrate your product or service in a way that can earn their business and, over time, their trust.

CONFIRMING COMMITMENTS WITH RELATERS

Relaters are slower, deductive decision makers. They listen to the opinions of others and take the time to solicit those opinions before making up their minds. So, make a specific action plan. Provide personal guidance, direction or assurance as required for pursuing the safest, most practical course to follow. Arm them with literature, case studies and any documentation you have available, because they will be "selling" your proposal to others within their organization. When you do reach an agreement, carefully explore any potential areas of misunderstanding or dissatisfaction. Relaters like guarantees that new actions will involve a minimum risk to their desired stable state, so offer assurances of support.

Try not to rush them, but do provide gentle, helpful nudges to help them decide (when needed). Otherwise, they may postpone their decisions. Involve them by personalizing the plan and showing how it will directly benefit themselves, their co-workers and the company as a whole. When asking for a commitment, guide them toward a choice if they seem indecisive. Quite often, they will feel relieved that you are helping them make the decision.

Another approach is to take the lead with Relaters. Once you have determined which action is in their best interest, lead them to the confirmation with your recommendation. When you have gained agreement, you can gently lead the Relater to the next step. There is nothing pushy or manipulative about this if you have studied your prospect's goals and pains. You are simply recommending the best solution that you honestly believe best satisfies their needs. You have created a win-win situation. Anything less is actually a losing proposition for this prospect... and for you.

There are four questions below that could be posed by a copier salesperson using *The Platinum Rule for Sales Mastery.* Now that you have read this chapter see if you can match the question to the corresponding behavioral style in the confirming phase of the buying cycle. If unable to do so, please turn back to refresh your memory so you will retain this important information when sitting before the next customer.

Here are the four questions:

1) "Which of the three copiers will work best to help your staff be more productive and improve your bottom line?"
2.) "Compared to the other copiers you have researched, which of our copiers most closely meets your specifications?
3.) "Which copier do you think your staff would prefer to use when they needed to make copies?"
4.) "Would you like me to prepare the necessary paperwork now that you have selected our most popular model by far?"

FOLLOWING UP AND FOLLOWING THROUGH

What is your "follow-up reputation" in your business? Is it 'always and promptly'? Or, "Usually fairly timely"? Or, "Doubtful it will get done"? The highest performers keep their promises and exceed the expectations of their prospects and clients. Be a bear about this one. It isn't a task to be dreaded; it is an opportunity to be seized. You can set yourself apart with good follow up skills.

What is the difference between "following up" and "following through"?

If your prospect declines or delays the decision to do business with you, you still have obligations to that person, which requires following up. If they do become your customer, you need to follow through; ensuring that every promise is completely fulfilled. We cover this thoroughly in the chapter entitled Assuring.

Let's take a look at the bad news first: No sale! Time for following up with this prospect.

First, the prospect deserves to be sincerely thanked for her time and for giving you an opportunity to exchange information. A hand-written note is always appreciated and sets you apart from a vast majority of salespeople that take shortcuts.

Next, you need to stop and objectively reflect upon the circumstances that caused the prospect to say, "No, thank you." Depending upon the situation, you may have a high likelihood of landing the account sometime down the road.

Here is a list of questions that you should ask yourself when debriefing each sales call:

- Did they decline because I proposed a solution before fully Exploring and Collaborating?
- Did I do my best possible job of asking questions; encouraging them to share their ideas, or did I do too much "proposing" of my ideas and possible solutions?

- Did I adjust to their pace?
- Am I confident that I helped them make the best possible decision that is in <u>their</u> best interests?
- By behaving respectfully and professionally, have I left the door open for doing business later if the situation changes?
- Based on their reasoning for not buying, might the situation change in the future?

True sales masters become comfortable hearing "no", as long as they have gotten to the real reason(s) for the answer.

After careful, objective analysis, you are now fully prepared to follow up with this prospect. We believe that in many cases you can often turn a "no" into a "yes" if you execute customized, long-term follow up campaigns.

It is common for salespeople to be in the right place (a qualified prospect), but at the wrong time. Many prospects, if empowered to educate themselves over time, can—and often do—change their own minds. However, no one likes to have to do so in front of a salesperson.

There are two different types of follow ups that you can execute; each serves a specific function.

The first is a standard type of follow up. The salesperson sends literature, case studies, testimonials and other "value proposition" information designed to further educate the prospect about the value your product/service delivers. Sometimes this does work, but no matter how cleverly disguised, it might convey a message similar to: "You didn't say 'yes' during our discussion, so here's evidence that may help you change your mind."

While this "traditional" practice of marketing is acceptable, it can be improved. Although educating prospects is never a bad idea, "attention erosion[1]" is making it harder to get your messages received, read and digested. Businesspeople today are over-taxed, stretched thin and have little time to spare reading your literature and newsletters.

However, we bring good news: The second type of follow up makes the first type much more effective.

Dale Carnegie taught us that to get what you want, first help others get what they want. He said that if we live our lives helping others achieve their goals; everything we desire will come back ten-fold. We heartily agree.

"Treat others the way they want to be treated," is the mantra of this book. By blending the Carnegie philosophy with ours, then adding a mix of cutting-edge technology, we were able to create a new method of following up with everyone in a customized, effective manner that ensures marketing messages are received with open arms (and open minds!).

Goal-specific Communication is the act of sending people (prospects, customers, clients, colleagues, referral partners, etc…) information that helps each of them achieve specific goals or seize a new opportunity.

If you take the time to ask interesting questions and pay careful attention to answers, you can now leverage technology to automate follow ups that send articles, tips and ideas to each of your contacts that match their goals, challenges, interests and preferences.

Pay careful attention to this statement: *If you send people helpful information—especially if it is unrelated to what you sell—you will position yourself as a helpful, thoughtful professional, and <u>not</u> as a predatory salesperson.*

For example: Let's say that Scott is calling on a sales manager and exploring ways to possibly help the sales team develop new skills and create more effective marketing messages. While Scott's company happens to provide solutions in these areas, he also discovers that the prospect is relatively new to his position and has not received formalized management training. Additionally, he learns that they invest large amounts of time, focus and money attending several trade shows.

After the sales call, Scott executes a "blend" of follow ups for this prospect. Using **The Cyrano Marketing System**, he selects a series of articles written by experts in the areas of interviewing, hiring, managing and interpersonal communications; all containing information that the prospect would find helpful in becoming more successful in his career. These are "relationship building" messages; chosen specifically to help this prospect become a more effective manager. These messages contain no information about Scott, his company or his products; they only serve to help the prospect.

When the prospect receives a few e-mails or articles mailed from Scott, he begins to perceive him as someone who is thoughtful, and also as someone who takes action on his ideas. As you might imagine, this type of communication begins building a bridge between Scott and each prospect.

When Scott calls back, he immediately offers to introduce the prospect to one of his colleagues that happens to be an expert in trade show marketing and long-cycle lead conversion. Couple that with the helpful articles on management skills, and Scott has earned the respect of his prospect by adding value at each touch point of the relationship.

More importantly, this approach dramatically increases the odds that when Scott sends "value proposition" information (literature, case study, etc…) that the prospect will read each message with an open mind.

By truly helping each prospect, Scott has <u>earned</u> "mind share" with each person. By matching messages to the goals, preferences and interests of every prospect, Scott eliminates "attention erosion". People in his Cyrano database actually anticipate his follow-up messages!

If Scott discovers that the timing is poor with a prospect, he "fills the time" by sending helpful information to him. If the prospect suggests that Scott call back in six months or so, he tells Cyrano what type of articles to send, when he wants them sent, and asks for Cyrano to remind him to call back at the appropriate time. In other words, Scott doesn't get frustrated when he is in the right place at the wrong time. Instead, he simply leverages this to his advantage. By filling the time gaps with showing the prospect that he cares about their success, Scott ensures that when he calls back, his phone calls are eagerly accepted and/or his voice-mails get prompt return calls.

As many thought leaders often remind us: In order to get everything you want, first help others get what they want!

While performing our sales training, we are often asked if adapting to different styles and/or sending helpful information may be "manipulative."

Our stock answer is, "It depends". If you do it right it is not. If you handle it with a win-lose approach it certainly can be.

If your intention is to help other people; help them make decisions that are in the best interest of their company and/or career (even if it means not buying your product or service), help them achieve more, help them solve problems and help them succeed, then you are in no way practicing any form of manipulation. You are living The Platinum Rule. You are leveraging the power of persuasion in a positive fashion to create win/win outcomes in your business relationships.

However, if your intention is simply to make a sale, mislead another person or do anything that is even 1% less than ethical, then we can confidently state that you are using adaptability, technology and persuasion in a manipulative fashion.

As Malcolm Gladwell pointed out in his best-selling book *Blink*, almost every person has the innate ability to detect authenticity in another person in mere seconds. As importantly, they do it on a subconscious level; without even knowing they are doing so.

If your intention is pure, prospects and clients will subconsciously be compelled to want to do business with you. Conversely if your intention is to make money, push people into making buying decisions and/or manipulation, then no amount of training, psychology or technology will help you build a long-lasting career in sales.

Here are some important questions you should pose to your sales manager and to your marketing manager:

- Are we effectively leveraging information gleaned from the field (sales calls)?

- Is our contact management system (or CRM) being used to full capacity?
- Are we effectively communicating with everyone in our database?
- Does every one of our prospects know about each product and/or service that we offer, and why they should be buying from us?
- Are we effectively cross-selling to each customer who makes a purchase with our company?
- Should we consider matching our benefits to behavioral styles of our prospects?
- Since it is now possible to automate customized follow-ups (even if salespeople forget), would we grow our sales if we added effective technology to our process?
- Do we have a system for developing leads, cross-selling, increasing customer retention and growing referrals?

These are very important questions for your team to consider.

While it is important for you to learn how to adapt to each prospect or customer during your sales process, it is equally as important for you to market/communicate effectively to ensure that you have a steady stream of qualified prospects, your current customers feel appreciated and thought of often, and you never lose another client due to perceived indifference.

[1] The Attention Economy: Understanding the New Currency of Business by Thomas H. Davenport & John C. Beck

12

phase 5
MAINTAINING RAPPORT
IN THE ASSURING STAGE

The greatest weakness of most salespeople is the way they handle the Assuring phase of the sales process. Most salespeople stop with getting the sales commitment; they disappear from the customer's life, leaving service, installation, training and follow-up to someone else.

One "old-school" method of selling has an adage that says the sale starts when the customer says "no." In direct contrast, we believe that the real job of selling starts when the customer says "yes." If you think about the lifetime value of a customer, it helps you understand how valuable this step is. Stew Leonard, one of the industry legends and head of one of the nations most admired dairy stores, operates on the belief that every customer that walks through his door is worth $50,000.

Leonard came to that conclusion when he realized that his average customer spent about $100 per week. Assuming a 50-week year and a customer lifetime of 10 years, the customer lifetime value becomes $50,000. Using the same process, smart car dealers place the lifetime value of one loyal customer at more than $300,000.

Assuring customer satisfaction is a secret ingredient of extraordinary sales success. You will benefit two ways by assuring each customer. First, this assures repeat business. Almost all products have a life cycle and will be replaced or upgraded. Customers have a tendency to return to the salesperson who previously matched them with a product that met their needs and then provided excellent service and follow-up.

Secondly, satisfied customers are excellent sources of referrals. Customers talk. They talk about poor service and they talk about extraordinary service. When they get super service, they refer their friends and relatives to the salesperson who delivered on his promises.

Without repeat business and referrals, a salesperson must constantly prospect and cold-call new accounts. That is not the way most salespeople want to spend their lives... and it certainly is not the best way to be successful!

When you start the sales process, you have a chance to begin building a good customer relationship. However, it is only after the sale, when you make sure your customer is satisfied, (preferably delighted!), that you really cement the relationship.

UNDERSTANDING CUSTOMER EXPECTATIONS

Top salespeople make sure they are positively clear about the customer's expectations... the criteria he uses to judge the success of the purchase. If you have executed the exploration, collaboration and commitment steps properly, you should be thoroughly familiar with those criteria. Be sure to monitor those criteria and stay involved. For many salespeople, this means they need a follow-up schedule. While every product or servicing cycle is different, there are standard follow-ups that all top salespeople incorporate into their sales process.

First follow-up: "Thank you!" note

Follow-up starts with a hand-written, "thank you" note immediately after the sale. It is amazing how many salespeople still overlook this simple step. Try it for a while and see how many of your customers mention it... or how many of your notes wind up on their bulletin boards or displayed somewhere in their office.

Second follow-up: Check-up

The next follow-up is just to make sure they received the product and that it is working. For instance, a computer salesperson might call five days after the sale to make sure that the system is performing the way the customer expected. This initial check-up call is especially important to recognize early on any problems or dissatisfactions. If the computer buyer has not been able to get his favorite software to work on your computer, they may be blaming you, the computer, your company, and life in general for a problem you could have fixed in five minutes. This call gives you a chance to preempt this problem before the potential emotional build-up that might lead to an unnecessary eruption.

Third follow-up: Gift

What better excuse do you have to contact a customer than to give him a present? Enhance every sale by following up within two or three weeks with a gift that represents a token of your appreciation... a little something extra. This should be something the customer did not expect to get and, ideally, it should enhance their product (or your service). It does not have to cost a lot but it should have a meaningful perceived value to the recipient.

For instance, a health club might give new members sweatbands with the club logo; a computer company could provide public domain software, monitor cleaner, or a diskette storage box. Management trainers sometimes take pictures of their training sessions and give the attendees and the person who made the decision to purchase the training copies of the pictures. The gift can be simple but should tie to the product and have a high-perceived value.

Important note: You may consider not sending or delivering any gifts to Directors or Thinkers. Remember that these people primarily focus on tasks, results and processes, not relationships. A well-intentioned gift may be perceived as "wasteful" or a "business bribe" and produce the exact opposite result you hoped to achieve. Additionally, some companies have policies that restrict or prohibit their employees from receiving gifts. A general rule of thumb (but not an absolute one) is to observe your customer's work environment. If you see items in their office with the logos of other companies, it's probably a safe bet that they would accept one of similar value from you.

Fourth follow-up: Referrals... the lifeblood for growing sales!

Here is an interesting thought about the book you just read: If you earn a referral from someone who trusts you to someone who trusts your referral source, you immediately bypass the Profiling and Connecting Phases of the sales process!

Stop and think about referrals you have previously enjoyed. Didn't the prospect immediately begin sharing information about his/her needs, their situation, their problems and/or their goals? Of course they did, because they trusted the judgment of the person that referred you to them!

When trust is implied, everything about the buying/selling process becomes easier.

How will knowledge of the four behavioral styles help you gain more referrals?

Let's consider this from all sides of the referral equation: The referring person has his or her natural behavioral style. The person to whom you've been referred has a dominant style. And, of course, you have your style.

How smoothly the referral process flows depends on your ability to "read" what happens between all three parties. For the sake of simplicity, let's call the person who refers you the Advocate. The person to whom you've been referred will be called the Prospect.

Here's where the behavioral styles come into play...

REFERRAL PROCESS WITH SOCIALIZERS

If your Advocate is a Socializer, you have some work to do to earn trust with this Prospect. Depending upon how strong of a Socializer, the Advocate might be referring many, many people to the Prospect.

Sometimes Socializers have a propensity for making referrals too quickly, and without fully thinking through if there is truly a great fit for you and the Prospect.

The Prospect, knowing the Advocate often "cries 'Wolf!'", becomes a little cynical about the people being sent his way. He may view you as "just another acquaintance of the Advocate", because he met ten other people referred from him during the past two months.

So, here are some great tips for helping you get better (notice we didn't say "more"?) referrals from Socializers:

- Ask for referrals the minute they have agreed to buy from you. When Socializers are excited about making a purchasing decision, they can't wait to tell the world. Let them!
- Example: "John, I truly appreciate your trust in hiring my firm for your marketing needs. We will run through walls to make you famous! I was just wondering if you know of any other business owners that might also need our services?"
  — Get ready to write… John will likely rattle off names faster than you can jot them down.
  — After the Advocate stops rattling off names, you might say: "Wow. This is some list. Thank you! I plan on calling all of these people, but I was wondering if you might glance over it and put a check mark next to the two or three that you think might be my best prospects?"
  — This will slow the Socializer down enough to consider the people on the list. You may find that he/she actually begins crossing a few off and narrowing down the prospects for you.
- Next, ask the Socializer if they would make phone calls to the prospects for you. Since they love talking on the phone and re-connecting with clients and colleagues, they won't mind your request to personally introduce you and discuss the work you will

be doing together.
- Personal introductions from the Advocate to the Prospect carry far more weight than you calling and saying you are doing business with the Advocate.
- Always aim for this outcome regardless of the style of your Advocate.

REFERRAL PROCESS WITH DIRECTORS

If your Advocate is a Director, you need to adjust the timing and process for gaining a referral.

First, we strongly suggest that you wait until you have successfully implemented your product or service and demonstrated that you are competent, reliable and trustworthy. Once you have delivered value for the Director, try this approach:

- Be direct and state, "Bob, I've done everything in my power to make sure that you have benefited from our relationship. I'm sure you might agree (pause until he nods). I'd like you to consider doing something for me that no one else could possibly do. Because of your connections and influence, you have relationships with people that would probably not give me the time of day. However, because of their respect of you and their high levels of trust in your business sense, they would easily grant me an appointment simply based on your recommendation. With your permission, I'd like to leave a small sheet of paper with my name and phone number at the top. Please keep it next to your phone. If someone pops into your mind that you think could also benefit from my product/service, simply jot their name down. I'll call you one week from today to see if you might have a name or two for me. If not; no worries. If so, great! Would you please consider helping me build my book of business?"
- Have the sheet of paper ready to go.
- If he agrees, call back in one week to see if he has any names for you. If so, say, "That's great, Bob. Thank you. I appreciate you

giving me both names. Because of your relationship, they would quite likely return my call if you simply called them first and teed it up for me. Could you do that? If so, I'll take it from there."

- Make sure that you follow-up with the Director and let him know what happened with each lead.
- Because Directors like efficiency, you may consider e-mailing a quick re-cap of each Prospect. Bob doesn't need to hear stories about how well it's going; just wants to know you followed up on his leads.

REFERRAL PROCESS WITH RELATERS

If your Advocate is a Relater, earning a referral takes time and effort. Notice we used the term "a referral" because one is all you should ask for!

Relaters guard their relationships closely, so take this into consideration. Also, just like with a Director, you should only discuss a referral after you have delivered on your promises.

Here are strategies to consider that will increase the odds that a Relater will refer you:

- Explain right up-front that the purpose of the discussion is to explore the possibility of getting a future referral from your Advocate (no surprises and no pressure).
- Let them know that you build your business from repeat customers and referrals.
- Remind them about how you treated them during the sales process: no pressure, no rush to make decisions and that you helped them make a decision that was in their best interest.
- If appropriate, remind them about the person that referred you to them.
- Assure them that if they were to introduce you to a friend or colleague you will treat them with the exact same professionalism as you did the Advocate.
- Show them your sheet of paper and ask them to think about

writing down one name and they may call you back at any time if they think of someone. Let them know that you trust their judgment and you will not be calling back to see if they thought of a referral for you. Don't bring this subject up again. If they call you with a referral, great. If not; let it go.

REFERRAL PROCESS WITH THINKERS

If your Advocate is a Thinker, earning a referral takes time and effort. As with Relaters, notice we used the term "a referral" because one is all you should ask for!

Thinkers guard their databases and relationships with their life, so understand that you're asking them to "open up" with information that they'd rather not release. However, if you earn a referral from a Thinker, you can take it to the bank!

Why?

Because the Prospect knows how thorough the Thinker is; if you've made it through his/her "buying gauntlet", you <u>must</u> be the best at what you do!

Thinkers guard their relationships closely, so take your time when discussing a possible referral. Also, just like with a Relater and Director, you should only discuss a referral after you have delivered on your promises.

Here are strategies to consider that will increase the odds that a Thinker will refer you:

- Explain right up-front that the purpose of the discussion is to explore the possibility of getting a future referral from your Advocate (no surprises and no pressure).
- Let them know that you build your business from repeat customers and referrals.
- Remind them about how you treated them during the sales process: methodical, thorough, no pressure, no rush to make decisions and that you helped them make a decision that was in their best interest.

- If appropriate, remind them about the person that referred you to them.
- Assure them that if they were to introduce you to a friend or colleague you will treat them with the exact same professionalism as you treated them.
- Tell them that they will not have to make a call to introduce you to the prospect; you will simply mention that you two are doing business together and the Advocate suggested that there may be a potential to work together. (The Prospect will be half sold when you mention that you're doing business with the Advocate. They will respect that Advocate's ability to select the best product/service.)
- Show them your sheet of paper and ask them to think about writing down one name and they may call you back at any time if they think of someone. Let them know that you trust their judgment and you will not be calling back to see if they thought of a referral for you. Don't bring this subject up again. If they call you with a referral, great. If not; let it go.

REGULAR CUSTOMER CHECK-UPS

On a regular basis (determined by the life cycle of your product), you should check with your customer to make sure they are happy and satisfied with the solution you have provided. This gives you a chance to identify problems and provides opportunities for follow-on sales and more referrals.

Immediately after the post-sale follow-up, we would recommend that you ask each customer questions similar to:

- "John, we often put articles or case studies in our newsletter, brochures and on our web site. You seem to be very satisfied with our product/service. I was wondering if we might be able to contact you in the future for your testimonial about our company?"
- "John, as you may recall, you found me through a referral from one of your friends/coworkers/clients/vendors. Because

of our excellent reputation for delivering on our promises, we are growing almost exclusively through referrals. Who do you know who _____?" Of course, you will describe your ideal prospect and prompt John's memory for referrals. We describe this process in detail in our upcoming book: "*Cyrano's Platinum Rule for Marketing.*"

• "John, I have found that it is much easier for me to keep my clients rather than running around looking for new ones. I am willing to work hard to earn your repeat business. I was wondering if you could tell me how, and how often, you would like for me to stay in contact with you over the coming months and years?"

If the customer is unwilling to give you referrals, you may be falling short of their expectations. This is a clear signal to review the product and the buyer's success criteria to see if they align. If you find an area where the customer feels like they have not received what they expected, you should acknowledge the problem and try to fix it. You might have to discuss all of their future expectations to make sure that you both understand the process. If you have not met some of their expectations, you should offer some type of "compensation."

Domino's Pizza offered us an excellent example of compensation. They had firmly established an expectation in the customer's mind that they would deliver a fresh, hot pizza to your door in 30 minutes or less. If Domino's could not deliver within that time, they took $3 off the price of the pizza. As we all know, they dropped the policy (due to their concern for driver safety), but their precedent was memorable, nonetheless.

If you are going to survive in today's highly competitive environment, you have to have an excellent product... and even better service. If you cannot meet the customer's expectations, you are not going to be in business very long.

This probably sounds like a broken record by now, but if you have a problem, you have to find out why. You have to talk to the customer to find out if their situation changed, if you failed to deliver what you promised or if the product was an improper match with their needs.

Sometimes, in spite of a salesperson's best efforts in the Exploring and Collaborating stages, a customer buys a product that fails to meet their needs. This is the very worst possibility, but the one thing you cannot do (if you ever want to do business with that customer again) is hide. None of us enjoys facing problems, but studies show that when a customer problem is addressed and rectified promptly, the customer is more likely to become a repeat customer than if the problem had never happened.

Problems give you a chance to show how much you care about the customer. To handle them correctly, you must immediately acknowledge the problem and take responsibility for your part in the problem. You then must to do whatever is possible to resolve the problem. This could be a letter of apology, partial or full refund, or replacement of a defective product.

You may have to return to the Exploration stage to discover what product solution would have met the customer's needs. You are trying to recover the customer's confidence and trust in your abilities to deliver a solution to their problem. Therefore, you must work through the collaboration and commitment stage again with them.

You are more likely to be successful if you have a sound strategy in mind for this recovery. You will probably have to make concessions in order to re-establish the customer relationship, but the rewards are worth the effort. At this point, it is especially important to keep the lifetime value of the customer in mind. Tape the dollar figure on your wall and stare at it while you talk on the phone with the customer. If you are face-to-face, jot the number down on the top of your note pad and glance at it occasionally as you listen. There is more at stake than the profit on just this one sale; all future sales and all future referrals from this customer depend on your ability to reaffirm your commitment to quality and service.

If the product was the right solution, but the customer still is not happy, there must be an expectation that was still unfulfilled. The reason for customer dissatisfaction in this instance usually falls into one of three categories:

1. PRODUCT FAILURE: Something has happened to the product… it is not working (physically or mechanically). This is what happens when a new car has a defect, but the customer will be happy as soon as the defect is fixed. However, it is critical that you make the correction swiftly and cheerfully.

2. IMPLEMENTATION: Sometimes, the product is working, but it is not working for the customer because the customer does not know how to use it… or how to use it correctly. There are probably thousands of software packages that failed because they were either too complicated to use, their manuals were hard to read, or the right training was not available. It may be an overly used word, but *user-friendly* is a key criteria for success. It does not matter how well your product works if the customer does not know how to use it!

3. BUYER'S REMORSE: Salespeople always underestimate the power of buyer's remorse. It comes from an uneasy feeling of guilt about spending the money, not being sure that it was the best decision or selective perception (when inordinate importance is focused on a small, annoying detail). For instance, a new fax machine works perfectly but has an annoying ring. Buyers expect their purchases to be perfect and having to cope with unexpected annoyances feeds their feelings of buyer's remorse.

When the customer is unhappy, we have to find out exactly why they are not satisfied. We can use the steps of Listen-Clarify-Respond-Confirm to make sure we resolve the issue. First, listen to the customer and restate the problem to make sure you both see things from the same perspective. Acknowledge the problem and define your responsibility. Offer an apology, even if it was just a matter of miscommunication. Fix the problem or offer compensation if appropriate. Ask the customer what it would take to satisfy them. Make sure the solution meets the customer's needs and expectations.

The real focus of the sales process is not gaining the commitment to the sale; it is providing service to your customer. Following the steps of Listen-Clarify-Respond-Confirm gives us a logical guide to making sure that the customer is satisfied with our product and service.

ASSURING CUSTOMER SATISFACTION WITH THE DIRECTOR

Directors usually do not look for personal relationships at work due to their focus on accomplishing tasks. With Director customers, do not rely on past sales to ensure future purchases. Follow up with the Director to find if they have any complaints or problems with your product. If they do have complaints, address them or the Director's natural impatience may motivate them to seek help elsewhere (probably with another company). As Willy Loman found out in *Death of a Salesman*, contacts mean nothing in an age that emphasizes change and product performance.

Impress upon your customer your intent to stand behind your product or service. Furthermore, you should stress that you will follow-up without taking a lot of their time. You might tell the Director, "You bought this to save effort and time. I want to make sure it continues to work for you. I will periodically check back to make sure everything is running smoothly, but I do not want to waste our time with unnecessary calls. When I telephone, if everything is fine, just say so and that will be the end of it. If anything is less than what you expect, I want you to call me right away and I'll see to it that the problem is fixed immediately." You may also want to offer a money-back guarantee. Whatever the promise, make sure you deliver everything you offer!

ASSURING CUSTOMER SATISFACTION WITH THE SOCIALIZER

In business, as in love, those interacting and impulsive Socializers frequently buy before they really know if it is the right choice for them. When they jump in too quickly, the probability that they may suffer buyers' remorse is higher than for the other behavioral types. Socializers can benefit from ongoing reminders that they have made the right purchasing decision because they get bored quickly, even with new things. Make sure you reinforce their decision by giving them plenty of service and/or assistance immediately after the sale. Be certain they actually use your product, or this type may get frustrated from incorrect usage and either put it away or return it for a refund.

Think of yourself as the organizer for a less organized type (any Socializer) to help them get the most use and value out of your product. As a bonus for the extra effort, remember that they tend to talk up or talk down whatever pops into their minds. Since they mingle with so many people, you can even ask them if they would be willing to share with others their glowing testimonials about you and your product or service. If they are feeling smart for using your product or service, most Socializers will give you more referrals than the other three styles combined!

Assuring Customer Satisfaction with the Thinker

Set a specific timetable for when and how you will measure success with the Thinker. Continue proving your reliability, quality and value. Make yourself available for follow-up on customer satisfaction and ask for specific feedback on the product or service performance record.

If you have tips for improved usage or user shortcuts, e-mail them to your Thinker customers. You should also ask for their ideas and opinions for how to improve your products and/or services. When they offer you their suggestions, get back to them about how your company is incorporating their ideas into future upgrades, revisions or new products.

Assuring Customer Satisfaction with the Relater

Practice consistent and predictable follow-up with the Relater. Give them your personal guarantee that you will remain in touch, keep things running smoothly, and be available on an "as needed" basis. Relaters like to think they have a special relationship with you, that you are more than just another business acquaintance. Remember, they dislike one-time deals, so follow up to maintain your relationship. Of all the types, they most prefer a continuing, predictable relationship.

Impersonal, computerized follow-through is not very appealing to this type, so continue building your business relationship with your low-keyed, personalized attention and offers of assistance.

Congratulations! You are now at the end of our book but before you get to work on practicing *The Platinum Rule for Sales Mastery* to become a more effective salesperson take a few more minutes to reflect upon what you just read about assuring customer satisfaction. First remind yourself that all customers – regardless of their style – deserve complete assurance that you are there to reconcile any problems they encounter with the products or services you sold them due to product failure, implementation, or buyer's remorse. Then remember that assurances will be more effective when they are adapted to resonate with the particular style of each customer. So take a few moments to complete the following sentence for each of the styles, "To assure customer satisfaction with _____ I must _____." Here is an example to guide your efforts, "To assure customer satisfaction with <u>Socializers</u> I must <u>be proactive in reminding them that they made the right purchasing decision because that style is prone to suffer from buyer's remorse.</u>" Now do one for a Director, Thinker, and Relater and you are truly on your way to reaping the benefits from those who practice the art and science of *The Platinum Rule for Sales Mastery.*

13

Sales Mastery On-The-Fly

This book has been primarily written for those who are focused on business-to-business (B2B) sales. However, ***The Platinum Rule for Sales Mastery*** can also be used by those who are in a sales position where there is little time to identify the behavioral style prior to engaging in the sales process... most likely business-to-consumer (B2C) or retail sales. This chapter has been added to the new edition of this book to enable those who work in a sales position that offers repeated, albeit narrow, windows of opportunity to interact with customers and increase the probability of making a sale using all the tools discussed in ***The Platinum Rule for Sales Mastery.***

One example of a situation where a limited customer interaction has not deterred novice salespeople from finding success is the semester-long sales class that Dr. La Lopa teaches at Purdue University (that contains a "hands-on" sales requirement). The class starts off with the students forming into sales teams (with about six members in each team to learn about teamwork) and then organizing themselves to accomplish the team's sales goals and earn the right to take part in an incentive trip at the end of the semester. The student teams then spend about four weeks working with Dr. La Lopa to conduct a marketing analysis identify one or two products that each team will sell during the semester.

While awaiting the arrival of the merchandise, the students establish price points for their merchandise and then use this book as their principle text to learn behavioral styles, adaptability, and the multi-phase sales process. When all is said and done, the students are left with about four weeks to sell the merchandise that they ordered. Although the students are encouraged to implement the five-phase sales process outlined in this book to move their merchandise, experience has shown that this not always works out (given their busy class, work and personal schedules). Students tend to use whatever time they have available to knock on the doors of sorority sisters, fraternity brothers, parents, friends, etc... Some set up tables on campus to connect with passersby's to sell their merchandise. They have learned to be successful doing sales mastery "on-the-fly"... and so can you.

Perhaps you are in a similar position yourself and knocking on doors, "dialing for dollars," or waiting for that next customer to walk into the store in need of your sales expertise. Remember the mnemonic device: CECCA

The first 'C' is Connecting; the critical first step that begins the process of learning the style of the customer and establishing trust and mutual respect. But how can a salesperson rapidly connect with customers when pressed for time?

The answer is to get into the habit of observing the behavioral cues that customers exhibit in order to identify their styles. Add to that a genuine commitment to engage in active listening and customers will quickly reveal their style to you even after making simple introductory questions such as, "How may I help you?" That is why it is important to use the Connecting phase to primarily listen and look for key words, phrases and nonverbal cues that reveal a customer's style to enable you to successfully move quickly into the next phases of the selling cycle.

Don't confuse "moving quickly through the sales process" with "high-pressure selling". A prospect may only need five or ten minutes to make a buying decision, but there's no reason why you shouldn't connect with them, explore their needs, work together on making a decision and assuring them. High-pressure selling is where you present products, overcome objections and use closing techniques to garner a sale. Our process is truly collaborative!

Consider the following scenario where a customer's behavioral cues could provide you with a preliminary insight as to his or her style. Imagine for a moment that you are a salesperson working in a men's retail clothing store and a customer approaches you.

You ask, "May I help you?" and the customer snaps back in a declarative voice that, "I need a top-of-the-line suit, I need it now, and I want a price below that of your competition!"

Or you ask the same question and the customer softly mutters, "I am comparison shopping to find a pair of sensible shoes that fits my budget and I would like to evaluate your selection"? By paying close attention to what the customer said and how he or she said it, we determine there is a good chance that the first customer is in a Directing mode (Direct + Guarded) and the second one is in a Thinking mode (Indirect + Guarded). Based on what you have learned to this point about behavioral styles, wouldn't these observations be good starting points for identifying their process for buying?

Imagine now that you are working a booth at a kiosk in a trade show and a customer engages you in a conversation. You cannot get a word in edgewise; she is more interested in talking about herself than asking you questions about the products you are selling. The next customer walks up and asks you direct questions about your product will give him a competitive edge over the competition and increase profitability. Thinking back to the descriptions of the four styles isn't it possible that the first customer is in a Socializing mode (Direct + Open) while the latter is in a Directing mode (Direct + Guarded)? Making a quick assessment and orienting yourself to the style of the customer enables you to adapt the pace and priority of the ensuing conversation to one that is amenable to the customer.

So, when attempting to make a quick connection with customers be sure to look for behavioral cues that indicate whether they are "open versus guarded" or "direct versus indirect" to form a preliminary snapshot of their style. This is also the point at which the "funnel technique" from the exploring customer needs comes into play as you begin to pose questions that will enable you to remain in sync with them through the remaining phases of the buying cycle.

Below are some sample open-ended and close-ended questions that could jump-start many transactional sales processes. Remember that the goal of the questions is to get a read on their style:

- Would you prefer I give you a quick rundown on the features and benefits (more Direct) of our service or walk you through the details (more Indirect)?
- Do you tend to make decisions more on facts (more guarded) or feelings (more open)?
- Would people who know you describe you as someone who is more competitive (more direct) or cooperative (more indirect)?
- When you see something you like, do you typically purchase it on the spot or do you prefer to wait and weigh more options?

Through trial and error, you will learn to develop questions of your own that will enable you to determine the styles of the customers you meet on a daily basis. Most of them will even appreciate any question you ask that is based on a sincere attempt to get to know them a little (learn their style) and uncover their needs. Besides, most people, regardless of their style, have had their fill of salespeople who quickly deploy high pressure sales tactics to make a sale. Your questions will immediately distinguish you from the pack!

Once you have mastered the talent for quickly connecting with the style of the customer, be aware that the remaining four steps in the sales process may very well unfold rather quickly with Directors or Socializers. Conversely, they may take longer if the customer is a Relater or Thinker.

What follows are some of our recommendations to help you use The Platinum Rule for Sales Mastery in a compressed time-frame when one-on-one with a customer. You certainly know your business and your customers better than we ever will, so these recommendations are meant to get your creative juices flowing to develop new techniques that prove to work best for you.

Once you are in the Exploring phase of the sales process (the 'E' in CECCA), the goal is to discover the wants and needs of the customer. At this phase of the sales process, keep the following points in mind for each style:

Exploring with Relaters	Exploring with Socializers
• Talk warmly and informally • Ask gentle, open questions that draw them out • Show tact and sincerity in exploring their needs. • They want to avoid confrontations, even minor ones. • Allow for plenty of time for Relaters to open up to you and reveal their innermost needs and goals. • The more time you spend Exploring with a Relater the higher the odds you will land them as a customer.	• Socializers get bored quickly • Strike a balance between listening to their stories and gathering the information you need. • When asking business questions, keep them brief. • Demonstrate how your product or service can get them closer to their dreams so they become excited about your product—and you.
Exploring with Thinkers	Exploring with Directors
• Thinkers don't care as much about social interaction, so get to the point. • Ask logical, fact-oriented, relevant questions, they will enjoy speaking with you. • Ask open and closed questions that investigate their knowledge, systems, objectives and objections. • Make your own answers short and crisp. • If you do not know the answer to something, do not fake it. Tell them you'll get the answer for them by a certain time, and then do it.	• Keep your conversations interesting by alternately asking questions and offering relevant information. • Directors want to understand where your questions are leading. • Make questions as practical and logical as possible. • Aim questions at the heart of the issue and ask them in a straightforward manner. • Only request information which is unavailable elsewhere. • Ask questions showing you have done your homework.

The next step in the process, as you recall, is Collaborating (the second 'C' in CECCA), where the salesperson gets the customer involved in the process of determining the best product or service solution that addresses their problem or need. Here are a few tips to keep in mind when working through the Collaboration phase:

Collaborating with Relaters	Collaborating with Socializers
• Show how your product or service will stabilize or support their procedures and relationships. • Present new ideas in a non-threatening way. • Provide them time to adjust to changes you suggest. • When change becomes necessary, tell them why. • Design your message to impart a sense of stability and security. • Relaters like to be shown the appropriate steps to follow, so share those with them. • Encourage them to give you feedback.	• Show how your product would increase their prestige, image or recognition. • Give them incentives for completing tasks. • Stress how their contribution will evoke positive responses from others. • Involve as many of their five senses as possible. • Show them how your solution will save them effort. • Back up your claims with testimonials. • Sprinkle in "visualizing future ownership" questions, such as: "If you were already running this software, how would you use it?"
Collaborating with Thinkers	**Collaborating with Directors**
• Emphasize accuracy, value, quality and reliability. • They dislike talk that isn't backed up with evidence. • Seek feedback by asking, "So far, what are your reactions?" • Present your solution that shows them they'll be correct in making the purchase. • Increase their perceived value with facts and data. • Point out the obvious negatives before they do.	• Your presentation must be geared toward their priorities. • Zero in on the bottom line with quick benefit statements. • They want you to do the analysis and lay it out for them to approve or reject. • Directors like rapid, concise analyses of their needs and your solutions. • Directors like being in control, so give them choices - then be quiet and let them make their decision.

Providing you have done a stellar job of adapting your sales efforts to that of the customer's behavioral style, you should arrive at the Confirming phase (the third 'C' in CECCA) often because you have adapted to the way they buy. Here are a few tips to help you confirm the purchase:

Confirming with Relaters	Confirming with Socializers
• Relaters are slower, deductive decision makers. • Present a specific action plan and provide personal guidance, direction or personal assurance as required for pursuing the safest, most practical course to follow. • Try not to rush them, but do provide gentle, helpful nudges to help them decide. • When asking for a commitment, guide them toward a choice if they seem indecisive. Quite often, they will feel relieved that you are helping them make the decision.	• Be open and ask, "Where do we go from here?" or "What's our next step?" • If they like something, they buy it on the spot. • Socializers dislike paperwork and details so they are likely to hesitate, and even procrastinate, when it comes to spending the time required on a contract. • Put everything in writing due to their tendency to be unclear about procedures, responsibilities and expectations.
Confirming with Thinkers	Confirming with Directors
• Give them both time and sufficient data for them to analyze their options. • When they say they will think about it, they typically mean exactly that! • Thinkers are educated, logical "shoppers." Know your competition so you can point out your advantages relative to what they offer. • Suggest a "Pilot Program" to reduce initial risks.	• With Directors, you come right out and ask them for a "yes" or "no" decision; in other words, deal or no deal? • Do not spend too much time discussing minute details. • Present them with two or three options and probable outcomes and leave the final decision to them. • While the Director is reviewing your proposal, don't interrupt them. The odds are high that they will find an option that appeals to them and close the deal themselves.

The final phase of the sales mastery process is Assuring (the 'A' in CECCA). Although this section is teaching you how to apply The Platinum Rule for Sales Mastery in a compressed time-frame, it is important to remember that we are not advocating high pressure sales which lead to a "one-shot sale." That is why it is important for each of the four styles to get the sense that you are committed to their long-term satisfaction and they can count on you for personalized service after the sale. This is what leads to repeat business and referrals. Consider the following tips:

Assuring with Relaters	Assuring with Socializers
• Follow-up consistently and as promised. • Keep things running smoothly and be available on an "as needed" basis. • Relaters prefer a continuing, predictable relationship. • Give them your cell number, along with an invitation to call you any time with any concern. • Impersonal, computerized follow-up is not very appealing to Relaters, so continue building your relationship with personalized attention.	• Provide reminders that they have made the right decision and plenty of assistance immediately after the sale. • Be certain they correctly use your product or they may put it away or return it for a refund. • Since they mingle with so many people, you can even ask Socializers if they'd be willing to share their glowing testimonials about you and your product with others. • If happy with your solution, most Socializers will give you more referrals than the other three styles combined!
Assuring with Thinkers	**Assuring with Directors**
• Continue proving your reliability, quality and value by continually measuring success. • Ask for specific feedback on the product or service performance record. • If you have tips for improved usage, e-mail them. • Ask for their ideas and opinions for how to improve your products and/or services.	• Do not rely on past sales to ensure future purchases. Follow up and address problems immediately. • Impress upon Directors your intent to stand behind your product or service. • Follow-up without taking much of their time. • Offer a money-back guarantee, if appropriate. • Make sure you deliver whatever you promise!

In summary, there is no reason why you cannot learn to apply The Platinum Rule for Sales Mastery in a compressed time-frame if you learn to apply this information to adapt to others. We are not advocating you adopt high-pressure sales tactics by any means; we are just trying to give you an opportunity to take full advantage of the few moments a customer may give you to convince them that what you have to sell will satisfy their wants and needs. If college students taking a semester-long class can learn to do it, there is every reason to believe that a full-time sales professional can do it, too!

Think back to the mnemonic device that represents the five phases of the sales process you have read a lot about in this book and how you can adapt The Platinum Rule for Sales Mastery in a compressed time-frame based on what you have just read in this chapter.

Another exercise you should consider doing is to take out a sheet of paper and craft the best opening statement or question that will elicit a verbal or nonverbal behavioral response that enables you to quickly connect with any style, thus increasing the odds of them purchasing from you. You may not get it just right at first, but after a few attempts you will succeed and enjoy the financial rewards that will come from adapting your selling style to match each customer's buying style.

14

take ownership
of your destiny

Imagine what would have happened if you had successfully applied the principles and practices of *Platinum Rule Selling* ten years ago... or even five years ago? Well, hundreds of thousands of people like you have already used these principles and experienced dramatic increases in sales volumes, more satisfaction in their dealings with customers and co-workers (family and friends, also!), and greater awareness of their own strengths and weaknesses. Many people report that they no longer feel like "just a salesperson"; they feel, behave and are treated like a *trusted advisor*. They have an increased ability to help people find solutions to their problems and are more adept at identifying new opportunities.

For you to also share in the pleasure from experiencing these benefits, we encourage you to get started this very minute. First, think about the goals you want to accomplish in the next year... the next month... the next week... even by the end of today! Develop a plan to meet those goals using **The Platinum Rule®** and the other principles that make up *Platinum Rule Selling*.

ACCEPT THE CHALLENGE

This first step requires your *personal commitment* to this challenge and *belief* in these principles. Their success is a proven fact and you can learn to put them to work for you. Of course, any skill takes practice, and you cannot realistically expect to put all of them into effect immediately. However, the minute you start to treat people they way *they* want to be treated, you will start to see immediate results. We encourage you to accept this opportunity to strengthen your selling competencies!

MAKE A PLAN

Once you have accepted the challenge, you need a plan to incorporate these techniques into your life. Although we have provided you with an extremely simple, effective method of identifying behavior styles, it does take some practice. That is why we suggest you complete the worksheets found at the end of this chapter to begin to incorporate what you have learned about behavioral styles into your sales activities. You will find answers to the questions posed on the worksheets by referring back to this book.

COMMIT TO GROWTH

"Change is inevitable... growth is optional." We love that saying because it's true. Right now, you have the option to "finish the book" and get on with the rest of your life and career. After all, this is close to the last paragraph. However, you also have the option to take this moment and make a life-changing decision. You may decide to *keep learning* about yourself; your strengths and weaknesses, your natural tendencies to react to both favorable and unfavorable conditions, how you make decisions, how you come across to other people, etc... You may decide to learn more about The Platinum Rule and apply your new knowledge in other relationships of your life... beyond selling to and servicing the needs of your clients: relationships with your co-workers, children, spouse and/or family.

Hopefully, you may decide to use this book as a jumping-off point for a new direction in your career. If that thought excites you, we urge you to visit our site: www.PlatinumRule.com and learn how The Platinum Rule may be applied in all phases of business: prospecting, networking, marketing, communications, customer service, referral building, client loyalty, hiring, management, leadership, etc… We offer programs, technology, books, CD's, DVD's, Brain-X self-paced mastery courses, speeches, and on-site workshops that are all specifically designed to help you apply this amazing concept in key facets of your business. There are also worksheets to enable you to establish a profile of each behavioral style and how to adapt your sales techniques accordingly.

May you walk the rest of your journey full of wonder and awe, and may you make many friends along the way.

Here's wishing you continued success!

Tony, Scott and Mick

Answers to Chart on Page 134

Directors	Socializers
• Be prepared, organized and fast-paced. • Greet them in a professional manner. • Learn and study their goals and objectives • Find out what they want to accomplish, how they are currently motivated to accomplish tasks and what they would like to change. • Get to the key points quickly. • Suggest solutions with clearly defined (and agreed upon) consequences… in addition to rewards that relate specifically to their goals. • Provide two or three "best bet" options (in writing if possible) and let them make the decision on the best course of action. • Make it obvious that you do not intend to waste their time.	• Introduce yourself in a friendly, informal manner. • Show that you are interested in them. • Let them carry the conversation; let your enthusiasm for their ideas emerge. • Be flexible in jumping to new topics that interest them. • Support their hopes, dreams and ideas. • Illustrate your ideas and benefits with stories and emotional descriptions that help them relate back to their goals and interests. • Give them dramatic, emotion-laden testimonials. • Clearly summarize details and direct them toward mutually agreeable objectives and action steps. • Provide them with incentives to encourage quicker decisions.

Thinkers	Relaters
• Be prepared, so that you can accurately answer their questions. • Greet them cordially and proceed quickly to the tasks at hand; do not lead with small talk. • Be willing to research answers to questions you cannot answer on the spot. • Hone your skills in logic and practicality. • Ask questions that demonstrate an understanding of their industry and reveal a clear direction of thought. • Document both how and why a benefit or solution applies to their needs. • Give them plenty of time to think; avoid pushing them into hasty decisions. • Point out the pros and the cons of your products and services; offering the complete story will build credibility. • Follow through on every promise… big or small.	• Get to know them personally; greet them in a warm, friendly (but professional) manner. • Develop trust, friendship and credibility in a relatively slow pace. • Ask them to identify their own fears and emotional needs after clarifying the tasks and/or needs of their company. • Demonstrate how your solutions will positively affect their relationships and help them better support their team. • Avoid rushing them; provide personal, but concrete reassurances as you move along. • Be sure to cover, point-by-point, how your offering is a complete solution. • Communicate with them consistently over long periods of time.

ABOUT THE AUTHORS

DR. TONY ALESSANDRA has a street-wise, college-smart perspective on business, having been raised in the housing projects of NYC to eventually realizing success as a graduate professor of marketing, entrepreneur, business author, and hall-of-fame keynote speaker. He earned a BBA from the University of Notre Dame, an MBA from the University of Connecticut and his PhD in marketing from Georgia State University.

In addition to being president of Assessment Business Center, a company that offers online, 360° assessments, Tony is also a founding partner in The Cyrano Group and Platinum Rule Group--companies which have successfully combined cutting-edge technology and proven psychology to give salespeople the ability to build and maintain positive relationships with hundreds of clients and prospects.

Dr. Alessandra is a prolific author with 18 books translated into 49 foreign language editions, including the newly revised, best selling *The NEW Art of Managing People* (Free Press/Simon & Schuster, 2008); *Charisma* (Warner Books, 1998); *The Platinum Rule* (Warner Books, 1996); *Collaborative Selling* (John Wiley & Sons, 1993); and *Communicating at Work* (Fireside/Simon & Schuster, 1993). He is featured in over 50 audio/video programs and films, including **Relationship Strategies** (American Media); **The Dynamics of Effective Listening** (Nightingale-Conant); and **Non-Manipulative Selling** (Walt Disney). He is also the originator of the internationally-recognized behavioral style assessment tool - The **Platinum Rule®**.

Recognized by *Meetings & Conventions Magazine* as "one of America's most electrifying speakers," Dr. Alessandra was inducted into the Speakers Hall of Fame in 1985 and is a member of the Speakers Roundtable, a group of 20 of the world's top professional speakers. Tony's polished style, powerful message, and proven ability as a consummate business strategist consistently earn rave reviews and loyal clients.

Contact information for Dr. Tony Alessandra:

- **Keynote Speeches:** Holli Catchpole:
  Phone: 1-760-603-8110
  E-mail: Holli@SpeakersOffice.com

- **Corporate Training:** Scott Zimmerman:
  Phone: 1-330-848-0444 x2
  E-mail: Scott@PlatinumRule.com
  Web site: www.PlatinumRule.com

- **Cyrano CRM System:** Scott Zimmerman:
  Phone: 1-330-848-0444 x2
  E-mail: Scott@PlatinumRule.com

SCOTT ZIMMERMAN helps companies *make more sales with less effort.* By combining proven one-to-one marketing, sales & customer service training with proprietary communications technology, Scott's clients enjoy measurable advantages over their competition.

During the past 20 years, Scott has studied graphic design, branding, positioning, psychology (as related to influence) business-to-business selling and one-to-one marketing.

In 1989, he started a full-service marketing/communications firm: Zimmer Graphics, Inc. In 2001, he unveiled the first web-based contact management system (called "Cyrano") that could automatically deliver customized messages to prospects and clients on behalf of salespeople and rainmakers. One-to-one marketing immediately jumped from theory to reality when The Cyrano Marketing System was released. Zimmerman promptly changed the name of his company to The Cyrano Group.

In 2003, Zimmerman began searching for ways to match marketing messages to recipients' personality types. His research led him to Dr. Tony Alessandra (one of America's foremost experts in applied human behavior). They began looking for ways to combine Zimmerman's new technology with Alessandra's proven psychology. In 2005, they formed and became become partners in Platinum Rule Group LLC.

Also in 2005, they co-authored *"The Platinum Rule for Sales Mastery"* with Dr. Joseph La Lopa. *"The Platinum Rule for Small Business Mastery"* was released in 2006 (with Ron Finklestein). In 2007, *"The Platinum Rule for Trade Show Mastery"* (with Steve Underation) became an Amazon.com best seller.

Scott has appeared as a guest on several video shows for TSTN.com (The Success Training Network). In 2008, Scott was asked to join the exclusive faculty of iLearningGlobal.tv to share his knowledge of leveraging psychology and technology for creating high-trust relationships. Scott is listed as one of the Founding Experts in the CanDoGo knowledge base for selling skills, personal development and motivation.

As a speaker, trainer and consultant, Zimmerman is known for his lively, humorous delivery while he gently leads people into a new way of understanding interpersonal relationships, the power of persuasion and how to leverage new technologies.

To reach Scott Zimmerman: 1-330-848-0444 x2 or e-mail: Scott@PlatinumRule.com

---

DR. JOSEPH "MICK" LA LOPA is an associate professor at Purdue University.

Dr. La Lopa currently teaches sales, management, and business feasibility courses in the Department of Hospitality and Tourism Management. He earned his Ph.D. at Michigan State University, his Master's at the Rochester Institute of Technology, his Baccalaureate degree at the University of North Texas, and Associates degree from Richland Community College.

Mick has a true passion for teaching. Within his first four years of teaching at Purdue University, he received every major teaching award that can be bestowed upon faculty members at the department, school, and university levels. He was the 2003 recipient of the John Wiley & Sons Innovative Teacher of the Year awarded by the International Council of Hotel, Restaurant, and Institutional Educators.

Mick has been happily married to his high school sweetheart for 15 years. They have been blessed with 4 wonderful children.

You may contact Dr. La Lopa via e-mail: lalopam@purdue.edu